Raw Notes

Claes Oldenburg
Raw Notes

Documents and scripts
of the performances:
Stars
Moveyhouse
Massage
The Typewriter
with annotations
by the author

2005 Edition

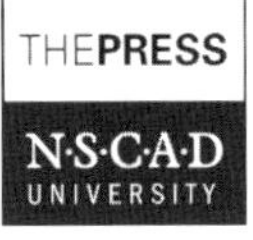

**The Press of the
Nova Scotia College
of Art and Design**

For Ellen Johnson

Cover: Claes Oldenburg photographed by Hans Hammarskiöld during the performance of MASSAGE

General editor: Kasper Koenig
Cover design: Jürgen Hoffmann
First edition production: Ilka Schellenburg
Second edition production: Arthur Carter, Paragon Design Group
Printed and bound in Canada

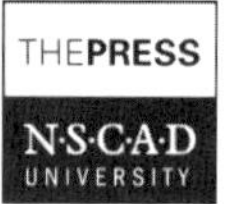

The Press of the Nova Scotia College of Art and Design
5163 Duke Street, Halifax, Nova Scotia, Canada B3J 3J6

Available through D.A.P./Distributed Art Publishers
155 Sixth Avenue, 2nd Floor, New York, N.Y. 10013
Tel (212) 627-1999 Fax (212) 627-9484

Library and Archives Canada Cataloguing in Publication

Oldenburg, Claes, 1929-
    Raw notes : documents and scripts of the performances: Stars, Moveyhouse, Massage, The typewriter / by Claes Oldenburg, with annotations by the author. -- 2005 ed.

ISBN 0-919616-43-7

    1. Oldenburg, Claes, 1929-. 2. Performance art.
I. Nova Scotia College of Art and Design II. Title.

PN3205.O4 2005   709'.2
C2004-906054-6

Contents

Preface

After each performance, all the documents relating to the performance were collected — down to the last scrap — and filed in a binder. The book consists of this documentary material, organized but otherwise unaltered — a sort of "found-object" approach, though the text has been extracted from its circumstances where it is sometimes not very legible. The look of the original is shown in the examples reproduced. None of the material has been rewritten for publication; all its peculiarities have been scrupulously retained. The aim has been to preserve the spontaneity of the writing and present this as a kind of style. The Notes can be read for themselves as well as for documentary purposes.

To maintain the feeling of informality, the text is typed rather than set and to further suggest the appearance of much of the original manuscript, it appears on only one side of the page. The text runs on without marking the beginnings and ends of pages in the original manuscript. Separate items and paragraph beginnings are indicated by dots.

Asterisks to the left of the text refer to the Annotations at the back of the book. The first number of the Annotation indicates the page; the second number the line. The lines are counted whether or not there is type on a line. Note: The larger asterisks to the right of the text on pp. 138-140 appear in the original manuscript and do not refer to the Annotations.

Clippings within the body of the text are reproduced actual size, wheras the reproductions of the manuscript pages at the back of the book are reduced by twenty per cent to fit on the page.

I am grateful to the Press of the Nova Scotia College of Art and Design for publishing this material according to my specifications — an unusual commitment. My special thanks are also due to Kasper Koenig and Ilka Schellenberg for their painstaking efforts on production. I have enjoyed working on the project and am looking forward to the possibility of publishing more "Raw Notes" from other periods with the Press.

Claes Oldenburg
Halifax, 1973

<u>STARS</u>, 1963, Washington, D.C.

- CLEANERS

- Ray Gun MAP in Washington, D.C.

- Welcome to R.G.T. in Wash., D.C.

- This is a town of initials, automobiles, and cleaners to mention some important things. Also long dresses + monuments. I will be asked no doubt in what way does what I do here reflect Washington. I was asked this in Chicago when I did Gayety there in February. Gayety was the name of a burlesk theater in Chicago, and the form of that piece (the form I say) was that of a burlesk show - ten minute segments with "clowns" and "dancers", and m.c. and so on. It looked very little like one I might add.

- My pieces have two titles, the first being one which describes the form of the piece, different every time I do a piece. Some examples are: Snapshots, Blackouts, Circus, Seance, Maps, Burlesk.

- The second title is the thematic title. For example the second titles of the above were: The Snook and the Streetchick; Chimney-fires, Erasers, The Vitamin Man and Butter & Jam (four parts); Ironworks, Fotodeath (two parts); Store Days, Nekropolis, Injun, Voyages, Worlds Fair (each in two parts, ten altogether, once a week); and Gayety (a burlesk thtr.) also Injun + Cleaners.

- There are also a number of subtitles. F. ex. in Gayety, which was devided into 8 sub-parts: Chairs, Eggs, Toast, Cigarettes, Ice, Fingers, Hammer, Finale.

- My pieces begin with the word and develop with the word because the word is the most concentrated way of suggestion, from which starting point a piece can spread into blooming. also a method of incantation.

· My pieces are always based on and the result of experience not ideas, which is true of all my work. My definition of what I want moves from ideas toward experience. In approaching a geographical piece like <u>Cleaners</u> in a place (like Washington D.C.) which I may have visited or even lived in (as I lived in Chicago) but never taken stock of physically for my purposes in making a piece, I begin with ideas - preconceptions, which form the first suggestive title.

· In this case there was none. After a visit to Washington for the purpose of using the place, I did form the title STARS, already more specific than the first stage. This came from seeing very clear stars in the sky on the last moment of my visit and seemed to concentrate certain physical properties of the place, f. ex. the patriotic motif. the radiated way the streets are built. But this title was still abstract in that it was achieved apart from a particular place in Wash. where the piece might be done.

· I returned two weeks later. This time, finding a particular place and increasing my contact with physical Washington by a tour of the whole city in car and other methods of contact, eating and sleeping in a certain area Etc. I was able to proceed to a more specific title. At writing this title appears to be workable, providing the place is available. My story can proceed no further until more particulars are added. Mainly the materials to work with - the available physical materials under the circumstances, perhaps found on the spot or borrowed or contributed, including

the people (at this time completely unknown) who will take part in the piece.

- CLEANERS is a title from a particular source, as the stars were a particular experience, which is the cleaning shop on the corner of P street and 21st Street (Aristo Cleaners). There is nothing about this severly white building, with black and red contrasts, the ads in the window, the signs, everything, that cannot have some part in my scheme. Even the name of the cleaners. That is because "Aristo" suggests both Greek subjects and aristocracy at the same time as by its typical abbreviation it suggests everyday vulgarity.
- In this the term is gesturing in many directions typical of Washington D.C.
- Washington is a white city as far as its structures are concerned. It is a black city as far as its population is concerned. Every effort is made to whiten the buildings and at nite they are lit up in imitation of the monuments. There is a desperate whiteness about the whole place, a bleached effect, which in fact is contained in the name of the city WasHIngTon, DEE CEE.
- This effect is very pronounced in the Washington Gallery of Modern Art, as it is in the National Gallery. The neoclassic white is a sign of position and importance, truth, morality, integrity of every sort. White is a powerful symbol in Washington, as it is in the Christian heritage. I am concerned with observing physical effects, not in interpreting them, by the way.
- There is no doubt that white is the color of the aristocracy, who

is no place as self conscious as in Washington. So it is fitting
that white should be the color of Washington and the color of a
Washington piece, or rather one of the colors, one pole, because
in fact half of the city is brown and black. More than half I wd
say and you deceive yourself if you do not realize the immense
tension between just these colors in the physical environment.

· Tension is the motive of art but unity is the thing to be sought,
a form in this case where the two poles of tension meet, a place
which has its own suggestive characteristics as form and color,
its own articles of activity and events and characters. This form
suggested itself first to me as a factory, a place where people
and things interact under certain circumstances. The place chosen
to have the piece in is the STAR RUG WORKS (or what used to be) –

* the earlier title thus occultly leading us. This might also be
called a Cleaners and the location is that of a factory and a
cleaning shop it lends itself to this.

· We have then at a Cleaners, which is a unifying form (everyone
send their clothes to the cleaners) an interaction of white shirts
and brown and black (employees), and the relation of the colored
to the white is generally through objects, especially clean
objects (which mean a lot of things between the two) and can cut
in the direction of several interpretations. The juxtaposition of
white and colored shirts is to be considered or of white employees
with colored shirts and so on. add military (khaki) clothes.
Potomac (water)

· On top of this we have the possibilities of steam and hissing &

not to mention the American mania for cleanliness and the historical and moral significance of cleanliness (as exemplified in the clean monuments of WASHington DEE CEE. Also SHIT and NOTHING).

· This is quite apart from the personal significance of the word and its suggestions, something I find more difficult to discuss. I have noticed that it contains my name (CLeAnErS) as Gayety contained the AE of my name, and I am aware that Cleaning as well as dirtying is an obsessive part of my subject matter.

· In this piece's preparation I have been repeatedly (as always) been made aware of the sponsor's ambivalent attitude towards the expectation of my making a mess and causing destruction. Cleanliness is an American theme.

· I will only say that my pieces wind up being very personal despite the attempt I make to come into contact with my surroundings and with others, to epitomize and typify the physical characteristics of my surroundings, I cant help, really must do it. It is suggestive effect of tension. I have no desire to make an impersonal work.

· I am using the city - the physical city as a huge palette of form and color, from which to take what I need - quite arbitrarily as I wd any material.

· A peculiar thing that occurs in my work is the desire to make a living thing with the pathos of having to resort to dead materials

· The fascinating thing about a person or any living thing, is that the object can be endowed with all the little evidences of life: intelligence, awareness, constant complicated movement & the contrast of this with the socalled inanimate...

- Loving life and movement I am always seeing movement even in the inanimate. I wish simply to create life, which is impossible as I go about it and the result is with my materials the illusion of life, comic or ironic or absurd. It becomes stopped movement or just the opposite of movement.

- This happens even when my materials are living things, people fex.

- To freeze in space is of course the very character of art, my method... Yet it is not love of art so much that has led me to this but love of the creation and handling of tangible substances, matter, matter with the illusion of life.

- Segal comes at this sculptors dream very directly which has its effects.. but the element of the method's resistance, the resistance or pathos of art is bypassed so that the pieces do look like calcimined corpses... I come through the ruses and ironies of art and produce my sensation of life by suggestion and surprise and other strategies.

- In a happening, double irony because the material is not inert, and it is necessary within my method (art) to make the material inert in order to give the illusion of bringing it to life. All the life of the person, by which I mean his imagination as well as his physical being, what can not be seen as well as what can be seen must be converted into objectivity or inanimateness, which I then (pathetically to be sure) bring "back" to life by my trix.

- My art is very much a language, in which some characters are fixed, some floating, some obvious, some secret - hidden even to

me (or especially to me). I always communicate no matter what.
I can always be <u>read</u>. There is 1. the thing itself (the word)
2. the juxtaposition or relation ("composition".. the sentence?)
Very common is a dramtc relationship of two objects in some context (space), by which an attitude or idea is projected.

- If I say I want a work to be personal that does not by this fact
mean pleasant. It means characteristic of the human personality
or one human personality and this is more likely to be eccentric
and devious. "Warm, personal" is an advertiser's cliche for something desirable. I see something much more complex and sinister
in the word.

- As a magician..really not cultivating or using my powers but inclined to disguise them, to hide behind some rather obvious dis-
guises..my theory has been that the power is the more effective
for being opposed by daily habits and acquaintances. Direct contact (DC) is too much.

- Now I am getting strange messages from Washington such as the
above & I have already determined that Denny is some sort of
magician..only Tyler knows me as the magician, but the power is
evident..

- My work has power entirely because it is magical and that is true
of what is miscalled my "theater" too, which is a way of casting
spells over groups... The Mystic Power Co.

- Theory

1. the main interest is form.

2. Everything is merely a pretext for form - there is no

relationship or meaning except form. <u>My use of form</u>

3. the properties of the objects + persons + situations are re-
    moved for my purposes.

4. This the third in series of formal pieces.

5. A Happening depends on material that is <u>on the spot</u> in a
    <u>particular place selected</u>. Even in Chi. chairs, mud sinks.
    Whatever was there.

- Thus <u>place</u> + <u>material</u> is absolute prerequisite for my happening –
  which is done not by preconception but <u>is an improvisation on what</u>
  <u>is there</u>. In "Sports" it was comb. of what was in my studio + in
  green galery. bikes, vacuum – hamburger fex.

- A neutral place will not do alone. A neutral place plus a place
  w. material.

- Dallas had both specific place + material.

- Chicago a more neutral place (illusion was necessary) + some
  material.

- A Happening is only as successful as the possibilities which
  present themselves – my invention is a constant.

- Happenings fail because of risks taken

- The Happening is a "play" of formal (+ physical + visual) effects.
  All elements in experience may be used, but these are viewed only
  for their formal (physical + visual) possibilities.

- The gallery becomes a specific place – "The Cleaners".

- end result of mine is not the simulation of reality but creation
  of unreality, magic, artificial reality, reality of unreality,
  dream

* · In museum, contrast w. be better. more effective.

· keep it small. very personal, very inclusive,

· personal in collision w. actual.

· This is a visual composition not a dramatic one. Or, the drama arises out of mood (a static condition) rather than action. This is a composition in which everything contributes to the effect. There seems to be little happening only if you do not interest yourself in detail or what is there. Thus, if the spectators merely entered and sat down + nothing took place, yet something would have taken place. However my intentions are not that absolute + this piece will be quite intricate.

· Almost everything I have bought in Washington is made in Japan.

* · The exoticism of Washington or (us) is not appreciated amid all these tapered columns + stiff horsemen. What a place of stores! Take 7th St. North, for example. The right bus ride is (presumably) the best happening.

· a display of objects.

· I am primarily interested in form but because I set no limits to what might be considered fit subject it appears I am more interested in other things. I am interested in all of physical experience both "raw" or stylized. There will be famous form - like cylinders, cubes, globes (in + out of various guises). There will be less famous form such as someone opening a letter or blowing their nose.

· This is a demanding type of composition + it is necessary to be patient, as audiences used to be. Today they must have their

"entertainment" and it must be immediate and simple.

- This piece is situated in the middle in many ways. As I think the perception of experience is. There is a doubt as to whether we are awake or dreaming and there is a doubt as to whether we are or are not existing in a composition. My method of composition may seem rigid at times and at other times not seem to exist at all. Throughout, the composition ought also to be (at) in the hands of the individuals in the audience. As for the use of familiar materials such as cloth or Wonderbread, this is so much form + nature under the present circumstances. Structure is as evident + as interesting in a Bacon Lettuce + tomato sandwich as in an apartment-building. I probably look more at food than eat it. There is always a dignity to form. One must not be distracted but pleased + amused by its occasional guises.

- The part played by the human being in this piece is first that he supplies a kind of unpredictable movement, which I like, to the machine that we have built. Second that he is interesting to observe, in himself, as form. Here again, I dont mean something narrow, like a life model, taking one ridiculous position after another, to be cast + set wherever streets join. I mean the observation of the whole human being - the translation wherever necessary of the invisible to the visible, the intangible to the tangible. The form, that is, of his feelings as well as his suit of clothes, his mental processes as well as the shape of his big toe.

- There ought to be nothing in this piece which can be said to be

unobjective or unobjectified. Where ideas or feelings or styles occur, they occur as facts + fragments in a composition which contains no more preconception or destiny than experience itself.

· As for its reflection of Washington, as a result of my own two weeks of preparation here, it is more my experience in Washington and this is also made physical + factual, which is why I speak of this piece as a "MAP". It is a very <u>personal</u> guide book + sightseeing tour - if that is what it is.

- A P O L L O Unites Classical and Negro (Apollo theater)

- Stravinsky made A musagete for Wash Society no?

- LO LO

- OL denburg

- PA t

- gLOria (who wanted to go to Apollo)

- RomanGreekNegroAngloSexualMarriage(United)Pageantum

- United (states) (negro-whites) Untied

- Three rayguns, one pyramid (obelisk), two cunt-mouth-assholes
  (capitols)
     A
- OLLO - classical facade

- Solo

- palm-reading - w. old songs

* - OURANG - OUTANG

- sex + power in neoclassic setting

- the train highest point on plain

- DIAMONDHARD CHROMIUM CO.

- ANOTHER CUSHIONED LOAD

- MAJOR ZIPPER CO.

- am. landscape all fantasy

- POE - TIME

- WISEACRE (D.C.)

- MOB (VOTING)

- ZERO

- STARS PLANETS SOLAR SYSTEMS UNIVERSES GALAXIES MOONS

- WAR

- TAPS

- PARTY

- EGGS shiver LIKE TITS (BUTTOCKS)

- LANGUAGE IS TOO SILLY FOR WORDS

- POPPY MADE MOMMY STOP KNITTING.

- A TRAIN TRIP

- AT 34 I GREW UP + MY FANTASY BECAME REAL. I WAS WHAT I PREVIOUSLY ONLY THOUGHT I WAS.

- THE DREAM.

- A SHORT STORY IN HIGH EXCITEMENT

- SOMEONE TAKES NOTES — READS THEM.

- DEER FOUNDRY

- FISHMAN WOOL PULLERS

- DYE WORKS.

- POE — R-GRILLET

- CAOUTCHOUC

- egg roll

- AUTOS

- INITIALS

- CLEANING

- Rocket

- Starlite

- Champagne

- posters

- program statement

- pink sheets

- cast-mimeo

- capitol wash mons + all rolled off roller as shirt as suit etc.

- <u>CLEANERS</u>

- STAR RUG WORKS. P ST.

- The very inclusive single word. not just cute.

- INSTITUTE FOR DEAF

- SOUSA (BRIDGE)

- Baltimore is never seen either by train or car because of tunnels.

- PAT BLOX

- WC Fields

- Greensburg.

- red devil

- red + green lights

- GUILT - DICK DICKIE

- Julian plays squash.

- HANDBALL

- SQUASH

- UNIVERSAL SCHOOL OF TRUTH

- AMERICA ON WHEELS

- KALORAMA

- HAWAIIAN BEAUTY SCHOOL

- LAWANDA SCH OF BEAUTY CULTURE

- DRY CLEANERS + DYERS

- WET WASH

- LAUNDRY FOAM

- 89¢ SHIRTS SUITS

- Aristo cleaners

- red + white

- red cleaners signs

- SPECIAL

- <u>Machinery</u> <u>factory</u> <u>WHITE</u> FACTORY LAUNDRY steam hoses - ir. board.

- Negroes in relation to white thru laundry cleaners.

- stars and stripes on piano

- Flamingo WASH

- MUST BE FORMAL BASIS

* - <u>Red</u> dress Cairo bag

* - Washington - crotch

- money made in Wash. MINT

- engraving

- water runs down side from eyes.

- bus backs in

- bugle call

- Scrunches

- SPRING at HOME

- MILITARY

- POLITICAL

- Plane flying over

- from Basement

- Camel TEST PILOT

- people seated around on benches

- party game

- music.

- Bird calls

- pigeons   crows   morning doves   birches   pines   CROWS

- deflated erect

* - hgs - hate success - are anti about everything.

- obstacle dance

- condition of country

- overalls

- POOL

- every society

- den

- pack

- bridges

- WAX Museum

- foggy Bottoms

- Paint can

- bubbles

- man of sea

- architecture.

- french rev.

- missiles

- peacock room.

- Tan - pink

- Khaki

- defense

- white - paper marble

- shoe shine
- stairs
- Negro.
- nuns - starched
- Ben Franklin + kite
* - Spt. 76 (Kaprows hap.)
- Dos Passos
- fried chicken
- Shrines - Mt. Vernon
- Cemetery
- Union of states
- Smithsonian
* - I J Mon.
- purple - yellow
* - Margot + tent.
- Underpass
- M street
- carbarn
- Am gall.
- market
- garage
- Boat Club
- Va.
- J.F.K.
- R.S.V.P.
- V.I.P.

*   ·   R.I.P.

*   ·   D.A.R.

  ·   AAAAAA

  ·   flour

  ·   cement

  ·   Baffles

  ·   old market

  ·   patriotic paraphenalia

  ·   parties

  ·   hostesses

  ·   invites.

  ·   INITIALS = POWER

  ·   FDR

  ·   FE DE RAL

  ·   Fol De Rol

  ·   POWER (NOT MONEY)

  ·   Sunken Mt. Vernon.

  ·   White swan

  ·   JAPANtrees

  ·   crabs   clams   oysters.

  ·   DUPONT underpass

  ·   sunk boat

  ·   lemon yellow white black.

  ·   HE SITS

  ·   Stars are lites in dark in which one may read an arrangement.

  ·   are convergences   are radiations (streets)   are cemeteries

      are birds

- Baseball stars

- movie stars

- WASH. Sts. – circles – stars

- crossings: old lady, pepsi, woman, cart, later cripples

- Lower East Side sequences of effects

- banquet

- painted model

* - Emilio

- Pat

- girl tatood

- cymbals

* - POP MUSCHINSKI

- P.O.

- Pat tatooed

- Mermaid.

- walls

- stars

- Achievement banquet

- (obelisk) emerges

- CAGE

- CAKE

- faces of oilcloth

- plastic comp for

- MILK

- cigarettes

- oil cloth

- plaster of Paris

- Love - jamas

* - MIL Explosions (bombs)

* - SPR birds + calls

* - POL?

- parties - stars of tables

- obelisk and shadow - RG

- tie

- for pop show: pillows

- postcards

- mailer

- bring up comix

- people in crunchy costumes

- roll

- multicolored waterfall

- Easter

- advance w. clouds

- thunder. wringing + snapping of towels

- big bride small groom

- down carpet roll rolling

- record cab calls

- WasHIngTon

- whites + browns.

- MILITARY.

- NEGROES

- POTOMAC
- 24 = 6
- 25 = 7
- 26 = 8
- Initials!
- secretaries
- all great grand notions at last clear down to what can be done +
  it is not bad.
- claesic   cleaners   classic
- clean = right white
- "clean" design - flag - emblem - wash ptg.
- flag = clothes = table clothes
- P (ie) (ee) St.
- peas on fl.
- people tied up
- the shower
- bird calls (Spring)
- cherry B time
- grey paper
- silver ink
- * write palmer method
- chalk
- Donald Duck
- * FED
- USA
- D.C.

- DEUCY

- Easter bunny

- Kids on vacation

- Civil War

- underground

- protocols

- cliff dwellers

- Brewery R of Wis. — under Freeway

- E.A. Poe Masque of RD

* - POW PLT

- have been in farcical frame of mind for a year

- serious farce is my natural form

- BLUE REALTY

- Wash exp has been farcical — once this is realized

* - all Dines were farces

- MUSIC

- dog bark

- girls join sing off key

- <u>Pat</u> licks lollipop

- cut brastrap

- a way of reconstructing the actual world to my liking.

- It is necessary to cope with (include) everything. (possess)

* - "Here is a whistle thats as much fun as a circus. Its a new slide

* whistle by Trophy Everyone can play it — (hes.) it has a wide tone

range. get up your own band — its as much fun as a circus — and

only 33¢..."

- genteel curtain to violence

- Resistentialism

- made in place + a method of contact + inspiration

- a community activity + teaching act.

- Launder Koin

- US Slicing Co. Inc.

- Pat singing gospel.

* - "release me"

- commercials

- record street sounds

- HOSTESS CUP CAKES

- JAPAN

* - "HIGH + MIGHTY"

* - "follow you"

- STUFF

- 1. Either a place <u>with</u> <u>material</u> - STAR or 2. <u>objects + costumes</u>
  made for a more or less neutral place. (clean happening) but this
  * could be a clean or resistant place greeng Lex. Hall. Museum.

- CLEANERS

- I WO jima - get larger stick more on it

- Colorful clothes

- TRAMMEL up in yarn

- DRAW TISSUE + plastic from Hamburger   spread on floors

- SPRAYERS AGAIN

* - ALLEY CAT

- A TRAY FULL OF ICE CREAM CARRIED THRU

25

- Carriage w. many colored doll babies tips over. put back full of radios too. pushed by a chintz face.
- very long leg pajamas.
- TOYS ARE WRAPPED AND TIED. goes back to other room to get. brings wrapped Back.
- <u>DEMONSTRATOR</u>
- straws in glass
- butters initials
- TATOOED
- MONEY.
- transformation dance.
- blows nose
- obstacle dance?
- ORANGE faces
- WAR – FIGHT
- several loud records – PAT SINGS
- MAN reaching into BOXES thru small holes.
- COCKTAIL PTY
- MISS WASHINGTON
- cleaners
- letters on legs.
- objects cover objects.
- Pat tatoo. + sing

26

- RELAYS (cold, noisy)

- red yellow blue oil cloth mats

- baby carriage

- sprayers again.

- easter grass.

- colored plastic scrims

- india tissue

- toys repainted (spray)

- golf umbrella.

- colored (painted) doll-babies

- flags.

- hamburger.

* - BLT.

- chintz (Hecht. fabrics)

* - shifts (5fl.)

- separate 3rd fl.

- 2nd fl. kids

- dresser - taffeta sheers.

- yarns

- military sounds

- loud records

- shouting

- Iwo jima in very colorful costumes.

- heavy pieces lifted + moved

- Miss Washington - down stairs. finale

- ties

- wonderbread

- Table oil cloth

- money

- demonstrator

- obstacle dance

- ourang outang

- initials

- LAUNDRY SIGNS

- Crossing – walks

- tatooed or painted person.

- oil cloth faces + pajamas.

- bride + train

- flamingo wash

- green hoses

- HAWAIIAN MUSIC

- ladders

28

- RELAYS (black)

- perfume - sprayers

- flowers - plastic

- silverfoil

- enigmatic objects

- dressing table

- extension lights

- bells

- beans.

- stools.

- purple cellophane

- sparklers

- gold jersey.

- blue w. yellow disks

- fans

- mirrors

- whistle

- commands.

- blind + deaf

- lights in eyes of audience

- feathers

- cube w. xmas lites

- 2 skip ropes

*   - quick come-to-lifes

- foot lights

- masque of red death

- bird calls

- bugle call

- cocktail party

- pool.

- suds

- palm reading w. old songs.

- organ music

- <u>drawing 'stars'</u> on glass: birds cross star streets

- Lincoln's assassination

- erasures

* - record cab calls.

- turban + shawl

- table at ends gold. reset for ea piece

30

- STARS (objects)

- tables set at both ends

- Pat eats pie

- place is sprayed.

- scissors

- silverfoil fragments

- from stairs. carry up dresser and paraphenalia. Gloria.

- (operator + assistant is in stairwell behind glass. Loudspeaker)

- Gloria has (breast) bells on table or on floor. touches with

  parts of body. face. nose – makeup.

- big bell

- man in muslin bag is put on floor bag unrolled around corner to

  other end – unroller climbs in. they wiggle. crawl in + out –

  bring out enigmatic objects.

- Kid draws stars – on long bag from one room to another –

  audience's anticipation.

- lights are laying out. Gloria picks them up. walks w. lights.

  Pat = quick come-to-life w. mirror-dance

- scissors (answered by scissors)

- flickering light.

- drinking from bottles

31

- MONUMENTS (white. in spots quiet)

- ice cream - red gloves

- spotlites

- white oil cloth

- brown mattresses of muslin (potomac)

- balls + balloons

- white gloves.

- white plastic screens.

- plastic storm suit

- pillows (6fl.)

- laundry bundles

- people on stretchers

- swingers + clouds

- shoes filled w. plaster

- ice

- milk

- heavy clothes - hats ties shirts

- heavy flag.

- painting legs white

- paint flag white

- white wigs

- bandages plaster casts

- everyone chews gum

- vegetables

- falling scenes (snow)

- drooping off ironing board

- columns
- cannons
- fort.
- crawl inside or thru cloth tube
- oysters
- crows
- lemon yellow
- wash mon - down stairs
- huge tie - sew.
- opening letters
- heavy flag.
- huge searchlights go on.
- woman shakes out wash. monuments + irons them - washes them.
- CANNONS
- everyone opens envelopes letters
- ARRIVAL of WASH. MONUMENTS - all sorts + sizes + IWO JIMA monuments CULMINATING IN superprick + collapse of I.J. group
- * Cleaners between ea.
- everyone chews gum
- * slides - of altered monuments
- banging at windows. ladders raised outside.
- in back: matresses drop in stairwell
- come up stairs. in thru windows.
- Statue I man in storm suit stuffed w. pillows w. white gloves. takes poses, pours + drinks milk.
- Statue II Pat as Athena. takes poses. moving from place to place

ice cream on w. bandages on. red gloves. fingers in bucket –
lick. Cannons

- Objects on stretchers vegetables balls people carried up from stairs laid

- balloons black + white

- A word is used by all saying over + over again

- LAUNDRY PARCELS THROWN DOWN

- legs painted white flag painted white – on oil cloth spread out.

- A heavy man (Statue III) w. heavy clothing – tie shirt + etc. posing

- feathers fall

- shot! a man falls.

- cab calls.

- organ music

- sparklers.

- many flashlites tied together. shine in audience eyes.

- bugle call interrupted

- bells

- covered w. suds

- feathers – lima beans

- skip rope first one room then another.

- end CLEANERS

- drum solo w. white stockings

- NURSES

- phonos.

- store the objects?

- <u>films of swimmers</u> Fix-machine mask film
- legs - come up stairs stockings sewn together
- handshake - gloves in long long sticks.
- faces - out of the wings.
- 2 people w stuffed suit lay out stuffed clothes as in window.
  pull apart w. string
- suntan faces
- man sleeps - thats all.
- blue candy bags
- grab newspaper - so - drop.
- a big ice cream bar
- shaving cream on lapels.
- man puts on sock after sock - then cuts them.
- balloons - yes - no. yes, no.
- <u>sound</u> sax trumpet drum
- <u>smell</u>
- MASKS when seated
- orange faces underneath
- foam rubber cut pies. tie on balls.
- <u>singing</u> throwing wonderbread.
- Wheaties.
- Capitol - bell
- Shouting
- violence of loud noise
- people carried in on stretchers
- fans

- drummer swingers
- I use human power
- milk
- white balls.
- soft heavy balls.
- erection that droops
- heavy flag
- heavy shoes - filled w. plaster ptd black.
- heavy ties
- heavy clothes filled w. sand.
- stockings
- hats
- bags
- the monument.
- flashbulbs.
- lamps
- puts on sand stockings
- pours sand.
- mirrors
- paints legs white   rifle   whistle   military sounds   commands
- 3 speakers for each floor   one over all - from control   20 min for ea. part
- blankets
- racks - for lights
- paint flag white
- Negro white

- scour

- blind deaf

- Iwo jima - cleaners

- white wigs

- bandages

- plastic casts

- boxes w. sand - wheeled in

- bags w. paving stones

- <u>Red</u> finale - girl down stairs in cost.

- Miss WASHgTON

- ice

- icecream

- white flowers

- one of ea - on ea floor thus 3 of everything

37

- GET:

- clock

- newspaper

* - rainbow posters

- Kraft paper.

- plank lengths

- saw

- cinder blocks

- TWO slide proj.

- TV

- <u>phonos</u>

- records: ALLEY CAT, I WILL FOLLOW YOU, RELEASE ME, ORGAN, HAWAIIAN.

- makeup: SUNTAN - ORANGE COLORED

- blue wrapping paper

- paint dolls

- typewriter

- costumes: plastic suit, white sox

- el. cords?

* - slides - Lincoln at th.

- sound records (or tape) cannons crows thunder

- bandages - strip

- food? + paper plates

- flags on sticks

- searchlight

- icecream

- chairs + benches
- yarn
- paint
- sign
- find oil cloth
- lights
- audience
- sound - records
- slides -
- paint rivers + tables
- incense
- blinkers
- stools
- scoop
- fix mon. nylon tape
- rearrange lamps - turn down some off
- paint tables (gold) stripes?
- TV facing away.
- searchlite stand
- lights outside windows ext. plug in.
- music from above. bugle call?

39

- <u>MONUMENTS</u>

- vegetables

- feathers

- pillows

- bandages

- ping pong balls

- <u>STARS</u>

- metal foil

- mirrors

- lamps - color bulbs.

- <u>CLEANERS</u>

- racks

- dolls

- kids cars.

- tricycles.

- <u>MAKE</u>:

*   - wheaties TUE

- monuments MON

- dress MON

- paint matresses MON

- hoods

- ice cream cake MON

· WASHINGTON - APRIL 1963

· Partial inventory of some objects and costumes etc. used in <u>STARS</u>:

· Four Capitol domes; 10 Washington monuments in size from six inches to thirty inches, of white oil cloth, stuffed slightly with foam rubber having the feel somewhat of fish. To be ironed and dropped off an ironing board to which bells are attached underneath. Iron is a small toy variety about five inches long. Eight plastic combs, various colors; a plastic bowl; jars of yellow and green vanishing cream; talcum powder; a plate of white soap and other toilet paraphenalia on a low round table painted green, of a strange appearance, with a drawer in it containing hairrolls. A circular mirror with two faces (one enlarging) on a table stand. A towel w. a picture of White House.

· Tights sprayed with paint in a tatooed effect topped by a tunic of Washington souvenir scarves. Around the head, stripes of blue, white and red in the form of a flag tied with a blue band around the head like a Salvation Army cap, mixing with long hair.

· Five suit coats, two striped; one black tuxedo; one white tuxedo in whose pockets are mirrors, hung on a birdcage stand on which also a bag containing makeup materials (labeled "Riggs Bank") and a white framed mirror.

· Certain objects sewn for the piece:

· A red dress made of four bags of red broadcloth hung over shoulders by taffeta bands, stuffed with paper, covered with pink polyethylene fabric. made to fall off by the untying of a bow.

41

- An icecream bar 5' x 1' x 3' of broadcloth and muslin stuffed with paper.
- Three pieces representing Wonderbread about 40" long x 20" high of multicolored disk broadcloth, stuffed with paper.
- Two striped ties 12 feet long of broadcloth stuffed with paper.
- Washington Monument replica of white oilcloth 12 ft long having 3 sides, each 15".
- Capitol replica in the round stuffed 40" diam x 60" high (not used).
- Three 20 ft. pieces in 4 ft. segments of muslin stuffed with paper
- Black "beard" for "Abraham Lincoln".

- Certain objects bought for the piece:
- A number of pieces were bought and not used in the piece, serving as mascots or leading to other objects or the result of wrong intuition. Such as 25 dolls (painted red yellow and blue); a red and white baby carriage; a dressing table of chrome tubes and with a circular mirror. A number of Wash. souvenirs such as three statues of Mrs. Kennedy and three mugs showing the president and family; 50 practice golf balls; four smoke bombs; a quantity of pink easter grass; several packets of toy money; an orange oversize baseball bat and green ball; two bow and arrow sets; a toy helicopter; a bird cage; a pair of black and white shoes; bubble pipes; etc. etc.

42

- Partial list of objects used in the piece:

- Three orange spray-guns; three bottles of incense: two types of air-purifier (one pine disinfectant); 50 Colgate soaps (white); ten American flags; one ice cream scoop; a styrofoam icecream container; six footstools; a pair of rollerskates; a quantity of clothing and shoes from Goodwill Industries and Volunteers of America; certain records ("Windup Doll"); a film on the capitol; slides of the Wax Museum and other sights; a set of girlie slides; a toy toaster; twelve whistles; bells; four toy cars whose wheels and pedals were removed.

43

· <u>W E I G H T</u>

· A happening for Washington

· 1. Light 2. Heavy

· R G Theater 1963 A Theater of Form

· <u>Stars</u>

· 1. dim 2. dimmer

· classical dark

· <u>Cleaners</u>

· 1. clean

· 2. cleanest

· white, pink

· <u>Weight</u>

· 1. light

· 2. heavy

· yellow

· ING/WASH/TON

· STARS/CLEANERS/WEIGHT

* · hpg for Washington - 3 decker.

· <u>Cleaners</u> accumulation of <u>white</u>. These illuminated - Pat

· <u>Weight</u> (Monuments) accumulation of <u>weight</u>. Then covered - Gloria

· <u>Stars</u> accumulation of <u>light</u>. rays set up to shine in faces -
   <u>Claes</u>.

44

- The Street

- The (Races) (games) (relays)

- 6 tracks.

- Preliminaries

- 1st (Race) (stripes) walkers sprayers, pies, bells, statues, lights, mirrors, objects; Acts, incl. lying. 15 min.

- OCCUPATIONS

- 2nd (Race) (stars) clothes, whistles, commands, fallings, (assassin), initials, tattoos. 15 min.

- Relays TEAM

- 3rd (Race) (cleaners) mattresses, stretchers, ties, toys + carriages, demonstrators, trays. 15 min.

- PARADE

- 4th (Race) (monuments) w. stairs. heavies, ironer – mon. ints, boxes, babies (all colors.), transformations. Ends with pile. Girl steps out of dress and leaves. 15 min.

- sound whistles organ music MUZAK birds cannons bugle calls drums demonstrator cab calls commands

- R E L A Y S

-   E L A   S – (CLAES) – (CLEANERS)

- R   A Y   (ETY)

- R   A S (STARS)

45

- RELAYS

- matresses

- walk w. thing, sit, other get up - right away - later.

- eating

- dressing - change clothes   loving

- Chris - walk w. ice cream

- <u>obj</u>

- toys

- Gloria color babies

- <u>FASHION</u>

- <u>PARADE</u>

- parade objects

- <u>dress</u>

- finale girl: Mary or big girl, if not Olga

- pile girl out of dress + leaves

- <u>OCCUPATIONS</u>

- ironing MONUMENTS

- plastic

- Cindy, joan, Cathleen, w. rivers

- <u>obj.</u> to do with

- Sandwich comp. for 2 (4) islands (beds, tablecloths) and stairs
  (up + down)

- soft objects

- result - 2 paintings.

- 3 complete setups how brought in? covered w. sheets. table w.
  food, white heavy

46

- D<u>ISTRICT</u>

- <u>TRANSIT</u>

- <u>PLAN</u>:

- Recurring fragments on a bent stage. SHAMBLES. MELEE.
  ANIMAL ACTS. Simultaneity. Fast pace. Alternation. free +
  casual coming + going Brief 45 min. at most.

- EVERY PLAYER has 2 or 3 actions WHICH HE REPEATS TWICE OR THREE
  TIMES AT GIVEN TIME INTERVALS, IN DIFFERENT PLACES
  SIGNAL FOR END. —

- an audience too expert at boredom to enjoy boredom.

- <u>method of organization</u> WIPE?

- walk thrus. drags pushes rolls runs passings vehicles.

- silent walkers variety of paces cards given to them fast slow
  changes

- word walkers

- stop + go walkers

- clutchers love walkers

- handshakers

- eat walkers

- dress walkers

- lift-walkers

- carry walkers

- break-walkers.

- bend-walkers.

- light-walkers.

- drink walkers.

- sing walkers.

47

- JA PAN

  April 24, 25 1963

  830 PM

- J A P A N

  (THE RACES, THE MERRYGOROUND)

  A FARCE FOR OBJECTS

  By CLAES OLDENBURG

  Made in WASHINGTON, D.C.

- JAPAN

  a comedy for objects in three parts:

  1. Relays

  2. cleaners

  3. Toy Riot

- ea. part about 20 minutes, the whole 60 minutes.

- a stage curving into rooms at a right angle to one another. The

  space of the W.G. of M.A. At both ends of the stage, a platform

  raised on horses w. steps leading to it.

- 1. <u>Relays</u>

- street sounds

- The platforms are treated as tables. oil cloth is taken out from

  under and spread on the tables - yellow for one, blue for the

  other. Table objects are all on the tables. This is done by

  flashlight. The floor objects are bought up the stairs - a flick-

  ering light in the stair well. A searchlight is set up in the

  stairwell to shine first into one room then the other. During the

  period of setting up there is only the natural sound of

the objects. Players having set up the objects now take the indicated 5 positions along the stage.

- water Buckets

- butter initials

- All this is done deliberately. When everyone is in their positions the operator blows a whistle and for one minute the players
work w. the objects at the positions. The table player exits.
fex. The whistle blows and the West table-player walks to the N
table. Every player moves up. The moves continue until the West
table player is returned to his place, whistles announcing each
change.

- At positions on the floor are: (in the center) a dressing table,
two hat racks w. clothes + objects + 2 small tables. ironing
boards When the players have returned to their original places,
big fans are turned on, one in each room.

- Organ music begins

- In the above piece there is an 'eccentric couple' - two dancers on
roller skates.

- 2. <u>Cleaners</u>

- drums

- This part is one of transportation. It begins w. a ponderous rum-
ble - first in one room + then another. Two large flat figures
(are unfurled like a stretcher) one from each room to be pushed
provocatively into the other. 2 players on stretchers are carried
up the stairs + back + forth along the stage up on the 'table' +
so on. Then the players are placed on the table stages (covered
w. plastic)

- sound of crows

- reaches into boxes

- The stretcherbearers leave + return, carrying: Wonderbread, the
Washington Monument, the capitol. While they are walking back +
forth (in bandages) three long mattresses arrive. Two down stairs
thru people, one over the heads, (thru window) These are placed
on the stage floor after being undulated in the air. The "bodies"
are chewing gum. From time to time they whistle (to each other).
(white on limbs?) There appear now: a Wheaties box (or ice cream
stick). They are turned in the air. Throughout the piece slides
of monuments are projected, first in one room then another.

- When the mattresses are on the floor there are some people under
them keeping them in motion. The monuments are on the mattress +
move also.

- The "bodies" open letters until their table tops are full of envelopes + letters.

- Amid this there are three free solo figures: a man who wipes the
monuments; a woman who tosses clothes (feathers) in the air +
takes statue positions.

- cannon, crows, thunder

- 3. <u>Toy Riot</u>

- bubbles, balls, clouds

- The audience is swept with flags on long sticks. The air is
sprayed w. incense and pine deodorant. The mattresses are turned
over to show the colored side. Toys are brought in, wrapped in

paper and string and piled on the tables. A tape is turned on
which begins w. Hawaiian music, Alley Cat + other records follows
w. Muzak, R + R + recorded stuff. Pat sing (recitals of lyrics).
Some of the toys are: a baby carriage stuffed w. Eastergrass +
radios, money and golfballs. Two large stuffed ties. food signs.

· The movement here is passing (coming and going) with meetings:
Carrying the several colored extension lamps, Pat will do an
'obstacle dance'. (tattooed, bow + arrows) There is an Ourang-
Outang (Poe). Several players wear hoods of flowered oil cloth.
Yarn is passed up + down. A tray of (ice cream) is carried thru,
held high. The unwrapping of toys begins. Crackling of paper.

· A girl whose hair is a flag is held rigid and raised by the
passersby who for this purpose wind themselves in blue cloth.

· This statue repeats and moves to center. The noise + action now
is extremely dense. From the floor above colored cloths drop.
Outside the windows colored lights go on.

· Assassination.

· Miss Washington descends the stairs in a vast red dress that
covers the audience, walks to center removes it and leaves by the
stairs. The audience in N. room will be encouraged to crowd in
for this finale.

· bring back.."Follow him"

· <u>instructions</u>

· Keep all objects + lamps high hold up.

· Keep rivers low + close to table

- no laughter

- dont follow tempo

- two min. in + out

- in other room!

- Charles only makeup

- GLORIA brush teeth + makeup - half fin. makeup? wash, STATUES, UNWRAP, STRIP makeup 2, screen star, photo - white

- PAT - DANCE + SIT IWO DANCE MONUMENTS DRESS W. SOCKS TATTOO.

- JILL - EAT, lying down, WAVE FLAG, UNWRAP dress?

- GAIL - IRON - MONUMENTS BLACK

- JOAN M. - EAT, IRON, DANCE W. WONDERBREAD TIES TIGHTS COLOR.

- CATHLEEN, JOAN F., CINDY, BETTE - RIVERS - BRING IN, CRAWL UNDER, UNDULATE - DANCE POP COST'S + STOCKS (white)

- OLGA - DRESS FINALE

- ED - M.C., OP. + LIGHTS Records TV Phono Searchlight Tape ANNOUNCEMENTS WHISTLE SIGHTSEEING (parody John Cage)

- CHARLES - TABLE, TRAY held up, DRESS W. SHIRT + PANTS TUX

- CHRIS - DANCE

- TOM, ALAN, CHRIS II, MIKE - STRETCHERS, WIPERS, SPRAYERS, IWO JIMA EAT ORANG OUTANG SLIDES NICE SUIT

- FRED - TABLE - WHITE SHIRT + PANTS

- GIL - DRUMS - SUIT

- (CLAES)

- Olga: In final four intervals descends stairs through people seated there causing them to get up, in a huge stuffed red skirt. She removes the skirt on center stage and leaves signalling end of piece.

52

- Cathleen: From under table right emerges (sometimes on, sometimes under) "river" of stuffed muslin, about 18 feet long.

- Joan F.: Same as Kathleen from under table left.

- Charles L.: 1. Makes up his face and dresses but is never satisfied. Takes off reapplies makeup redresses, etc. 2. carries a long oval tray full of plates with colored foam rubber through the act, on the 3 stages.

- Chris D.: 1. Dances on rollerskates with Pat. 2. Sits in a small chair and is shot repeatedly. His head falls after he attaches a little red star to his skin.

- Fred: Lies down on table (where icecream is set) Covers himself with plastic and opens letters filled with talcum. There are thin wires attached to his arms and legs and body.

- Alan R.: in a fantastic costume (orangoutang) of flowered oilcloth and muslin manipulates a 12 ft. replica of the Washington monument (which is soft) and two 12 foot ties.

- Tom, Mike: 1. spray the air with perfume, brush the floor and clean the Washington monument. 2. assist in the raising of Pat as the Iwo Jima monument.

- Chris H.: Assists in the I J monument. Operates slides.
  Ed: operates electrical equipment, makes announcement and operates other slide projector. Watches a film on Wash. D.C.

- everyone independent
  Ed: his ACT IS TO TURN ON AND OFF: THE 2 PHONOS + 2 TAPES + 2 RADIOS + TV. + FINAL (?)

- GIL: just goes + drums

<u>MOVEYHOUSE</u>, 1965, New York

54

* · SKISS UNO

· ice cream cone

· burlesque

· blow up screen. let air out.

· mattresses all over audience

· SKINNY MOO TEX

· SKINNY MAWTECH

· CHINGA MAW CHOTEX OKEX

· CHINNY MAW KOTEX

· CHINTZY

* · EXPANDING VAGINA

· EXPANSYVAGANZA

· BY CLAES OLDENBURG short but Black and White expandsymaganza

* Cinekotek (x) XX Lafayette St. Dec. 1, 2, 3 1965 also later?

Act I Claes Oldenburg Illustrated (C.O. Ill.) (Copyrite)

· ("STENCILS") "CUTOUTS" (blackouts)

· on certain chairs - instructions + costumes.

· like a game on some - none.

· numbers flashed on screen.

· Hawaiian music.

· scissors + newspapers - cut out p. so + so - that.

· something to eat - two pieces soft white bread. put picture

between bread. wrap it + place

· film screen is ripped apart in front of them. things thrown

on it.

· "audience" "spectators" shouts

- man w. hatchet hits w. wood, sits down

- helmet w. lights swinging light blinking pulled several

  connected

- KAZOO

- juggler. <u>faller</u> falls down stairs.

- whistling

- putting on makeup

- moon - on stick dom carries

- attaches string from eyes to screen one after another

- wrestles w. giant popcorn bag

- Dom. carries some obstacle.

- shoots gun - who

- Litterer, throws paper around

- Light match

- woman screams: "a snake!" "There's a snake on the floor"

- "Shut up lady"

- Snatches of conv.

- abstracted elements from reality composed

- remarks

- Johann becomes Santa Claus as he searches.

- Ellen - moves constantly.

- John - snores

- two people laughing crying screaming

- BOX office covered w. plastic

- Helene, posing

- Shigeko? on stage.

- smells of Lestoil hot bucket

- Mirror-head.

- w. plank or ladder lays out, crawls.

- Jo collect money w. tamb. on end of alum. stick.

- people come up - and down

- shout

- <u>burp</u>.

- keyed - one number means x to one, y to another, say a min. after
  cue.

- opens door, shouts 'hey!'

- popcorn

- arguments

- Letty covers person w. black cloth

- roll things up aisle

- dishes dropped on stage.

- King Kong. snarl. pick up doll

- John is King Kong masher

- enormous bag of popcorn + coke.

- S. Claus

- King Kong

- Magician

- stage - Jo laid out sleeps

- picks up girl

* - Fay Wray

* - FAYAWAY

- Seats are landscape

57

- Ventriloquist
- France
- Let all read cards <u>for improvise</u> or improvise from costume
- rope on aud.
- some way to signal group.
- scream
- run up aisle
- "don't worry about a thing folks" (person on edge of stage)
- in aisles
- hair net
- aud. - silver fans?
- dom. - several umbrellas. placed on seats? he carry
- Things - to be spoken?
- mark seats w. names? how organize? pattern?
- white bags. white cartons?
- Ellen - ghost
- Freddie Magician
- newspaper
- light matches
- Pat the laugher
- Johann talker Litterer
- dishes - Pat
- rope - seats
- rope - someone tie up someone?
- sound - chains on alum. ladder.
- breaking glass.

- <u>prop box</u>
- popcorn
- ice skates - Pat up on seats
- raquet
- fold out meas. stick
- whistle
- shoot silver gun - France, Jo
- silver helmet
- juggler front. Jo ass't w. mirror on head.
- M. Mouse hats
- tamb on stick
- lima beans in air
- pitcher of water
- add to this any special effects by me.
- taking kids out - fake baby.
- throwing pies.
- Ironing board broken
- Frannie - violin
- <u>cut into film</u>
- <u>Macys</u>.
- <u>commercials</u>?
- white gloves - usherettes
- white stockings - all.
- megaphone? - sp. eff. for John
- white chair - john - stage
- card table? painted

- silver scissors.

- silver ladders (alum.)

- pipes?

- hooks from ceiling - sp. eff.

- feathers in cone of light sp. eff.

- tell actors this is also very much a mood piece + subtle.

- whole point is to - like holograms, materialize subject (also like

  a _seance_ - a key parallel) + materialize the cone of light. fill

  with smoke

- much smoking before performance

- Johann finds objects which are hung up on (or held by) Ellen

- pipes - assembled

- white fur.

- raincoat

- balloons. - Canal St. - Vacuum - sp. eff.

- "Has the movie been on for long?"

- "Would you get me a coke?"

- "Psstt - what time do you have?"

- "I hate melodramas."

- "Ha Ha, 'ata gal, you show 'em!"

- S Claus

- drunk

- applause

- stomp

- clap

- whistle

- better torches.

- more bulbs on side

- megaphone + mickey mouse

- put legs up

- say "ssh!" w. meg. - John

- light match - ?

- put black cloak over head?

- tie chair to john?

- scissors to cut.

- Pat sings - MIKE

- John <u>juggles</u>. tumbles.

- Pat stands up and screams at me

- footlites on aud. or project several films at once on screen
  or slides pales it color + bw

- responsive reading by slides like sing along

- As Dom moves he sits in seat tearing newspaper into umbrella
  and chew gum

- fur coat on Santa - rent one.

- MOVEI

- The Moviehouse

- Mickey Mouse at the Moviehouse Movies Moviemouse

- The central figure (me) sits at table with typewriter and telephone behind is screen on which is projected image of me sitting at typewriter at table with telephone. The speaking I do is prerecorded on tape and played thru loudspeaker at back but I lip synch with it.

- There are two usherettes and four disturbers the latter are sitting in seats when people enter or enter with people They get up throughout the performance and obscure it by <u>removing</u> or <u>putting on clothes</u>. Get <u>popcorn</u> and <u>cokes</u> etc.

- <u>From time to time enormously loud movie music comes in some sound track</u>.

- Over me is shade which I can draw down now and then

- Usherettes just walk back and forth with flashlights <u>look for objects under seats</u>

- stiffened clothes bend out wires.

- Balloons or someone fat labeled Expanded Cinema

- Lecture on Expanded Cinema Usherettes blow up balloons to bursting wear bands saying Miss Expanded Cinema

- Phone rings all the time

- At side of stage films a screen on back of which is sprayed paint or such while light from projector shines on it or a Tsq film spliced together crazily or lizard battle repeating in a loop completely discontinuous

62

- Roar of Lion on tape from time to time

- Thousand balloons of Mickey Mouse blown by big fan in lobby

- equivalents for people? balloons in seats?

- blindfolds

- As the people enter, the moveyhouse is dark as it might be entering a continuous performance, in progress. piano is playing.
  also sound of movie track

- A rope is stretched around the seated area. There are usherettes
  with flashlights. spectators are seated in moviehouse seats

- The people are led up to the stage behind the screen and seated
  (HOW) by the usherettes. on "landscape" of boxes + cloth? FROGS
  Some seated in back.

- When all are seated a signal is given (Signal?)

- Using tall aluminium ladders in front of the screen the usherettes
  (unbutton cut w. scissor. RIP w. blades) the screen (or things
  are first thrown at it) or it is ripped down. THROW STREET BALLS
  (AT FIGURE?)

- The film now shines on the audience.

- The projector goes off. The lights are raised slightly showing
  empty seats.

- People who had been concealed under the seats rise out of them:
  Using flashlights or matches or turn on bulbs Lovers f.ex.
  LIPSTICK Spectators. dissociated action Man grabs his hat and
  goes.

- Coughing. applause. eating.

- Shouting (during film. one audience may think its the other.)

63

- They confront each other with the film screen between.

- Eventually all in seats move to one spot and then exit.

- Looney Tunes and end. Miss Kemp? (speeded up?) curtain closes.
  houselites up.

- usherettes - (min. one ea. aisle. one on stage) costumes. fold
  out for taking screen down?

- ticket taker -

- spectators - lovers - man - woman - child?

- pianist - LIZ

- Usherettes will in effect be shadow play

- How could seating of audience too be shadow play and substitute
  for film ie. while film is on weakly...a faded film or a film very
  pale with little doing...hmm

- Use of slide projector with stencils or fan in front to flickr?

- Something to be given the audience to cut out or tear what - For
  audience give them an image to eat. between bread

- Film: Reading a newspaper. Page after page, turning, or Magazine

- Or following someone riding a bike?

- John juggler silver balls

- Could severl films be projected at once on same screen

- Stencils effect - light one side, dark another, could be color or
  have color windows Mickey Mouse.

- at end all MMouse hats or just PAT + ME.

- Using the stage

64

- EXTRAVAGANZA a happening consisting entirely of the description of a happening with the license to imagine events possessed by poets

- Described by me wearing sunglasses seated like a commentator on stage at table with mike. Shining at me is projector either projecting blank, just light, or projecting my image (film with john at studio)

- Perhaps two assistants picking events description out of boxs behind me. Perhaps a group of players sleeping on stage or from time to time performing some vague action. Perhaps several describers in different parts of room a la "I have a lady here in the balcony" or walking with mike or commentators during an election or news event. But all imaginary.

- Could the audience be blindfolded or the scrim passed over them as before suggested.

- USHERS

- NURSES.

- everything in attendance but the actual event Emperors new clothes no film in camera

- Canned applause and laughter - crowd sounds - ssh!

- Need advertisement quick flier.

- Vinyl Raincoat

- MUCH SMOKING

- INDIANOLA.

- the sound of (?) low or hi

- blank film - w. a few frames of an image inserted here and there and a fan in front.

65

- LIZ PLAYS her melody when image comes - cues based on images.

- <u>shadows</u> from audience action.

- lights under seats. little bulb to hold. flashlites.

- incidents in audience

- 1. one person (JOHANN) always looking for something with aid of usherette (SHIGEKO). following another whom he constantly interrupts (ELLEN)

  2. one person a pickpocket (DOMINIC) - when he approaches someone they fall asleep.

  3. one person a "masher". A man putting arm around girl.

  4. a couple making love. (Claes + Pat)

  5. a person eating (JO)

  6. a person coughing (Raysse)

- <u>sound</u> - cues? when sound comes on - loud. <u>Cleopatra</u> fex.
  every five min. 4 times

- Ea. person sits down then + puts on their masks for a min. The light must catch them standing up. What if whole green is shot onto seats

1
2   } action - LIZ plays
3

4 - fanfare

5
6   } action - LIZ plays
7

8 - fanfare

9
10   } action - LIZ plays
11

12 - fanfare

13
14   } action - LIZ plays
15

16 - fanfare

17
18   } action - LIZ plays
19

20 - fanfare.

- Performance for Cinematheque Dec 1 2 3 1965 and Dec 16 17

- <u>Composition for Moveyhouse</u>

- MOVEYHOUSE Composition for a movie house, the 41st St. theater,
  Dec. 1, 2, 3, 1965 at 8:30 PM

- Usherettes (nurses): - Jo Eno - usherette - collection. helps
                            John blindfold, ice cream cone.
                          - Åse Lyttkens
                          - Shigeko Kubota
                          - France Raysse - ventriloquist. sit on
                            stageedge sit on chairs

- Piano player: - Liz Stevens

- Spectators: - Johann and Ellen Sellenraad. looking is con-
                  stantly blowing up balloons. hands to Ellen who
                  ties + ...?
                - John Jones - Santa - chasing Mickey Mouse
                - Dominic Capobianco
                - Claes and Pat Oldenburg - Pat - dishes.
                - Lette Eisenhauer - a smoking woman - Lipstick im-
                  print.

- Ticket Taker: - Fred Mueller

- The performance lasts about twenty minutes.

- PLEASE DO NOT SIT IN THE MOVIEHOUSE SEATS - FOLLOW THE FLASHLITES
  OF THE USHERETTES TO SEATING.

- AUDIENCE STANDS

68

* · <u>MOVIEHOUSE</u>

· by Claes Oldenburg

· A sculpture in light, time, and space using actual materials for the <u>Cinematheque</u>, at the 41st Street Theater, Dec. 1, 2, 3 1965

· Persons assisting:

Ushers:	Jo Eno
Spectators:	Lette Eisenhauer
	Fred Mueller
	Pat Oldenburg
	Ellen Sellenraad
	Johann Sellenraad
Doctor In The House:	John Jones (Juggler)
Pickpocket:	Dominic Capobianco
Piano Player:	Liz Stevens

· The piece extends about twenty minutes. <u>Audience is requested to stand at the side of the theater in the aisles and not occupy the seats.</u>

69

- The aim here is to evoke the abstraction of an actual movie theater with the addition of a certain amount of fantasy.

- Mood is extremely important, and I ask that the simplest actions be performed with respect for the sense of overall mood. The actions are simple because it is their appearance which counts and especially the overall appearance.

- When the piece begins the five Spectators and Dominic are seated in a row under the beam of the movie projector. The two ushers after helping arrange the audience along the side aisles begin to hand out cards on which are written simple instructions and a number which is to be counted out in the mind at a set rate, and gives the length of time for the action.

- These cards are to be observed with the small flashlights provided, as rapidly as possible.

- The white cards are given to the Spectators, except Dominic, the pickpocket, who does not receive any cards. At the beginning of the piece he starts to move through the aisles toward the stage end and there picks up and carries back to his original position the bicycle.

- When a pink card occurs, the usher must follow it and not give out any cards until she has finished her action.

- If a Spectator receiving a card is in the period of following the instructions of another card, he says "No Thank You", finishes his card and then waits for another.

- While waiting without a card, the spectator looks at the empty screen, or improvises in the spirit of the card instructions. A

reading of all cards is suggested. His improvisation may also be connected with a part of his or her costume, as f.ex. Pat, wearing ice skates is instructed to show them by putting them up on seat ahead of her.

· If you have not received a card for some time, signal usher. When she comes to you, pretend with her that you have lost something on the floor before receiving card.

· Always wait 5 to 10 counts before starting action on card after receiving it.

· After finishing a card move one seat to left or to right, alternating directions. When edge is reached, find seat in any other row.

· Do not give cards to and have no relations with John (Juggler) or Piano player or pickpocket.

· No cards are to be given out after Dominic, who is the timer has returned with the bicycle across the seats. He turns out the projector. The performance is over, and all leave, but not all at once. When all are gone from the theater, the piece is over and the houselights go on.

· Spectators and ushers receive flashlights and kits. In kits will be found material to use in certain actions given on the cards, as f.ex. popcorn to eat.

· 1. smoke

· begin by sitting in file

· 50 instruction cards.

· <u>RULES</u>

- each one has a tiny flashlite to read the card. Those who smoke, smoke constantly.

- cards are given out by 2 usherettes who are in constant motion.

- Also instructions to usher on red cards.

- Pickpocket is also in constant motion crouched down.

- Others look at cards surreptiously.

- If you are still in a period of a card say no thank you, and wait for another.

- in periods between cards, either improvise in the spirit of the cards or according to costume. Signal usher. In this case, pretend you have lost something, before following card.

- The action continues until Dominic has climbed over the seats w. the bicycle, reaching the projector.

- Dominic has watch, which he looks at w. his flashlite while going thru seats - never into aisle, climb over seats.

- light cards discreetly.

- any number may be included

- count always at set rate. If counting ends before action, sit down abruptly.

- move one seat to right + left alternately when sitting down after finishing a card. When reach edge find another seat in any row.

- everyone has same bag of props. Male and female group - May be exchanged. Everyone has overcoat or some outer garment.

- Collect tickets for next performance.

- final performance will be done without cards.

- always count ten at least before beginning action – wait longer if desired.

- Usherettes – whole pace should be slow

- any variation or combinations allowed.

- note usherettes do not give cards to Dominic or to John.

- The point is that the mood + place is more important than the action. the problem is how to stimulate an amount of action sub-ordinate yet complementary to the mood, in the 9 people involved.

- As usual, everyone is a discrete unit

- + also achieve flashlite effect.

- each person is individualized by costume.

- Always look forward after receiving card or at any time not engaged.

- When usherettes have card, they do not give out cards.

- Usherettes take time to hand out cards

- read cards fast

- while Dominic is going, everyone gets up + leaves he turns off proj. house lites on.

- John's and Dominic's actions re music etc. are described separately

- John (....?) + juggle + music.

- <u>props</u>: plastic bag.   theater kit.

    - bell (5)

    - mirror (5)

    - popcorn (5)

    - apple (5)

    - can of coke + cup (5)

    - handkerchief (5)

    - MM mask (5)

    - kazoo (5)

    - white gloves

    - matches

    - (cigarettes)

- Two of each - for audience

1. stand up + look behind. long - 10;   short - 5

2. move to person nearest you and put arm around him/her

   long - 20;   short - 10

3. stretch hands in air + yawn. long - 10;   short - 5

4. take mirror out of prop bag + look in it. long - 10;

   short - 5

5. take bell out of prop bag + drop it. long - 5;   short - 2

6. cough. long - 10;   short - 5

7. laugh out loud. long - 10;   short - 5

8. say: "get your hands off me!" repeat if necessary.

   long - 10;   short - 5

9. snore. long - 20;   short - 10.

10. move three seats to left. long - 10;   short - 5.

11. take out popcorn + eat it. long - 20;   short - 10

12. get up and go to washroom. (come back immediately sooner

    if counting ends) long - 20;   short - 10

13. put on coat + take it off again long - 10;   short - 5

14. get down on floor + look for something while mumbling.

    long - 20;   short - 10

15. applaud. long - 10;   short - 5

16. eat apple. long -10;   short - 5

17. open coke, pour in cup + drop can long - 20;   short - 5

18. scream. long -10;   short - 5

19. climb over seats to nearest person and sit down long - 20;

    short - 10

20. stand up + say: "I've seen this picture!" long - 10;

    short - 5

75

21. cry in handkerchief. long - 10;   short - 5

22. whisper very loud: "I wish I knew how this ends!" repeat.
     long - 20;   short - 10

23. put on white gloves, holding hands up. long - 20;
     short - 10

24. put on mickey mouse mask. long - 20;   short - 10

25. blow kazoo. long - 5;   short - 2

· USHERETTES

1. cross aisle shining flashlite down long - 20;   short - 10

2. walk quickly to stage. up stairs, out on stage + straighten
    curtain. long - 20;   short - 10

3. stand in the light of the projector + slowly turn around.
    long - 10;   short - 5

4. look under the seat of the nearest person with flashlite.
    long - 10;   short - 5

5. comb hair. long - 10;   short - 5

· Ush Kit

· Translate France's to French.

76

1. RECEIVE CARD

2. COUNT TO FIVE

3. DO ACTION COUNTING

4. MOVE ONE SEAT TO LEFT OR RIGHT

5. SIGNAL USHER OR INVENT YOUR OWN ACTION

6. WHEN USHER COMES, PRETEND TO LOOK FOR SOMETHING ON FLOOR WITH
    HER

7. RECEIVE CARD, ETC.

- IF YOU ARE IN THE MIDDLE OF AN ACTION WHEN USHER OFFERS YOU A
  CARD, SAY "NO THANK YOU" AND DO NOT ACCEPT CARD.

- REPEAT ACTION IF COUNTING IS NOT FINISHED. WHEN COUNTING IS
  FINISHED, STOP ACTION EVEN IF IT IS IN THE MIDDLE OF THE ACTION.

- WHEN USHER OFFERS YOU TAMBOURINE, SAY "SORRY I HAVE NO CHANGE."

- WHEN ONE PERSON DOES ONE OF THE FOLLOWING, DO IT ALSO:

SAYS "SSHH"

APPLAUSE

LAUGHS

SAYS "QUIET"

PUTS ON MICKEY MOUSE HAT

SAYS "TSK TSK"

COUGHS

- SMOKE AS MUCH AS POSSIBLE.

- DOMINIC SIGNALS THE END OF THE PIECE. WHEN HE PASSES YOU WITH
  THE BICYCLE YOU MAY LEAVE.

77

- Instructions received from Ushers by Audience (Players) of

  Moveyhouse based on typical behavior in film theater.

- Stamp feet

- Scream

- Step on a Paper Cup

- Smash Porcelain Cup

- Stand up and drop all your props. Pick them up.

- Wipe your face with a Handkerchief

- Put on your coat or take off your coat

- Eat potato chips

- Stretch arms in the air and yawn

- Say: "Quiet!"

- Climb over seats to nearest person

- Put arm around person nearest you

- Put your feet up on the seat in front

- Shine a flashlight in your mouth and pick your teeth

- Stand up and look behind you

- Pour Coca Cola in a Paper Cup

- Eat an apple

- Move out into Aisle and into next Row as if the Row was full of

  people.

- Say: "Get your hands off me!" (Repeat)

- Say: "Sssh!"

- Blow Glitter

- Say: "Aw, I saw this picture!"

- Move to nearest Newspaper. Pick it up and read it.

78

- Look for something lost, on hands and knees.

- Move to nearest Newspaper, pick it up and dust the seat.

- Cry in your Handkerchief

- Move three seats to left

- Whisper: "I wish I knew how this ends" (repeat)

- Move to nearest person and say: "Who do you think you are?" and hit them in the shoulder with fist

- Shine flashlight in your eyes and hold down lower eyelids

- Laugh

- Say: "Tsk, Tsk.."

- Cough

- Rock from side to side

- Say: "Mom, I want another piece of candy."

- Stand up quickly, as if a mouse under the seat

- Say: "Pardon me."

- Put on the Mickey Mouse Hat

- Applaud

- <u>For ushers</u>

- Cross from one aisle to other

- Sit on the edge of the stage

- Comb hair

- Walk to stage, straighten curtain

- Look under a person's seat, making them get up

- Stand in the beam of the projector and slowly turn around

- bicycle?

- leave papers on seats

- larger handkerchiefs

- John - Fantasy figures. cue Liz

- move among and as doctor w. stethohand feel hearts

- say "AAH!"

- blow up balloons

- Light parts of face and touch them.

- When the House Dr. comes, relax bandage arm

- <u>Reminders</u>

- Translate Frances cards

- Ushers kit.

- Replenish all Kits.

- do people stand up move talk enuf?

- what special effects needed?

- length of counts?

- Dominic - leave bike w. wheels spinning = film = mickey mouse = fan.

80

- On first visit to theater find it a real place, a charming obsolete silly little theater. Was used for recitals by students using Wurlitzer instruments. Rudy tells me he played there.

- Rauschenberg points out that no scenery is necessary. I agree.

- The sensitivity to place however has a radical influence on my performance. Rauschenbergs and Whitmans develop stage oriented with seated conventionally placed looking forward audience watching "the picture".

- Weakness to place makes me think of the whole place as participating. The audience only an element. The charmingness of the place is a circumstance that makes the performance possible.

- The performances from _Autobodys_ on (1963) characterized by supersensitiveness to place and to circumstances - more empty, the place itself doing the work (like water lapping), less imposition from me. R-berg and Whitman from this vantage point seem theatrical. Former supporters deplore change no more Artaud and frothing.

- But R-berg and Whitman look a kind of court performance, all decorative.

- I think of the 5 cent theater (not any more) on Third ave. near 14th St. and of the pickpockets in cheap theaters.

- a story from Milwaukee, a friend watching movements of pickpockets late at night among sleepers in the theater

- To physicalize - by which I mean make material - the cone (Ice Cream-Illinois Central cone) of light. Light comes in cones, like ice cream. To physicalize, realize, actualize...this cone,

proceeding from the projector. Like hoops of growing diameter.

- · The fan. Also functions as chopping instrument - as with sausage
or any meat the basic delineator of three dimensional or material
space. The fan and then the wheels of the bicycle, from a happy

- inspoturition wheels of same revolving more slowly the outer end
of the "spot" (projected, ejaculated, castuponwaters "spot" Pro-
phylactic jection. Ject - throw). Anyhow. As usual..the unity or

- echo of form: equizzilents: Fan-Proj.-Cycle-Circ. Mirrors.

- Does noone enjoy this play of form as I do. This powerful in-
spired indifference to all but formal relation. Mozart.

- · Our "Oats, Beans and..what?" Our little night snota Snotta

- · Moviehouse should be expanded - it is expansible - to Academy of
Music or some big theater. Audience in bleachers on stage drinking in the beauty of the actor watching the selfcentered crawlings
of the vast audience...

- To me film is as abstract as painting...to physicalize this. to
suspend it in space this, this far...in front of the screen halfway hologramic..

- people (cli....?) as they grow old - in re to their _own_ (physique)
environment.

- A movie or movey house or micky house mousey mouse or..is simply
a moving or movey house (audience) or a group of completely sepa-
rated people constituting a whole...image of life to me...in
motion. Not still sitting like in usual movie house but here

- screen still-sitting and aud. movz.

- Marvelpusthings are...merely filmed

82

- The props are mythological + repeat - fex. chair.

- The props are recurrent symbols: chair bike umbrella...simple

  objects around

- the themes are recurrent - lack of touchability isolation

- annual xmas piece.

- Variation - handcuff spectators

- Moviehouse - composition for disks and circles

- Rules or principles such as to use an object or wrong thing

- second piece a variation of this say "fantastic" rather than

  "realistic"

- Fan - devil

- Fan Tan - gum - mug

83

- Script etc. of <u>Moveyhouse</u>

- <u>The spelling of the title</u>, as above, to emphasise the pieces
  concern with moving things and to suggest Mickey Mouse, Saint of
  the Film, double of myself, the object with ears: projector and
  camera.

- <u>Integration of the piece with other work at the time</u>:

- At the time of this piece, I was preparing my one-man show held
  some mos. later at Janis Gallery (March). Residue of the summer
  was a concern with rotation of choppers as expressed in the Fan
  Object.

- The flickering effect obtained by putting the Fan in front of a
  projection of light (simulating the film flicker) integrated fan
  object with situation and its objects (Moviehouse).

- Fan - Devil (Swe.)

- Formal theme of piece: disks and disks-in-rotation.

- Necessary and desirable, to integrate performance with other work.

- Some disks in the performance:

Mickey Mouse Ears

Reels of projector

Bicycle Wheels (slow turning)

Half circles, arches at sides of Moviehouse

Paper plates used as fans by Audience (Marked Fan)

Mirror on Head of Doctor in the House

84

- <u>Iconography</u>. "Strange Mickey Mouse" a geometric form of MM originally intended as model of "Popular Museum". Krazy Kat architecture. Not used in advertising. Compare to Film camera which was Character (logo) of <u>Fotodeath</u>, 1961. Light that does not kill, projects life - the film. "Annihilate-illuminate", Ray Gun Slogan. Life thru light (fire).

- <u>Circumstances</u> (preliminary)

- A "happening" for me is all circumstances. Created by circumstances. Result and fruit of circumstances.

- I have agreed to do a piece to benefit the Filmakers Cinematheque, a piece on the theme "expanded cinema" which as the series develops, comes to mean what Higgins later labels "intermedia", or the mixture of film, live, lights, sound etc. (Basis later for a form of nitespot)

- As usual becomes necessary to define my position in relation to "intermedia", "happenings" - as represented in this case by Bob Whitman's <u>Prune Flat</u>, and dance "happening" (or what) - the Rauschenberg group. (spawn. The cluttered scene.) My work does not stand still. Friends of earlier work are not friends of present work and v.v. Complicated by confused reports or none at all, hearsay.

- <u>Position now with re "happening"</u>

- The original happenings were non-professional, in that they required no special skill. Only one skillful person necessarily involved, who obtains, organizes, but especially <u>perceives</u>. Concept of my hapgs 1961 was as a way of showing How I see. That is, the

professionalism (if offhand) of Artist. But dancers actors not necessary. In fact <u>not wanted</u> What was wanted: the suggestiveness of raw action.

· Effect of happening depended on audience feeling and seeing as I did..."professionalizing" audience vision (like drugging audience?) Audience including players.

· · (Billy says "teaching" today is more shaping of "perception" happenings in that way didactic)

· Audience is not passively watching a spectacle

· A "teaching" period could be a series of happenings or series of happenings could be a "teaching" period

· Professionalisation of happening effects is not possible (unenlightnd curiosity might come) because no real skill is involved, so might just as well be children playing or audience standing on street corner not paying $2.50

86

WHAT IS A HAPPENING?

For the last 2 weekends, 946 people experienced Robert Whitman's Theatre Happening and involved themselves in the bizarre art of mixed media. They saw film, projection, the movement of live men and women, costumed only in vinyl, performed to recorded and live sound. They saw much more.
They saw a Happening!
It will happen again this Fri., Sat., & Sun. at 8:30. We suggest you experience a Happening yourself by calling for reservations.
MARTINIQUE THEATRE
32nd & Broadway   PE 6-3056

- Pandering to unenlightened curiosity

- If professionalism is introduced, dancers, the result is not happening but "dance theater"

- OK professionally but without unique definition

- So hapng is never professional. It is a demonstration by the "artist" or the "perceiver" For me consequence of thinking so is that happenings are not my main activity, but incidents of pressing my vision closer to audience or making more public. like a monument.

- The part of my work which is placed in public context is the theatrical part, the "happenings", in which the aim is an active exchange of my attitudes and sensibility with a living audience. The end is less perfection, as in the sculptures, than action, process. A "happening" is always imperfect, and the audience bears part of the responsibility for this type of public monument.

87

· In deciding when where and how to do a happening im under no
obligation to act professionally. Rather the opposite: to wait
for all the right elements to assemble

· happenings are not my professional activity, relief in fact from
professionalism

· Normally a happening is fragmentary: movable isolated events but
playing with unity has produced for me "theater" effects unity of
mood, theme, even plot was played with imaginary settings plot
and stereotypes were treated as objects manipulation is not <u>with</u>
the desire (logic) of the thing usually but against it, to dis-
locate (so for example plot was chopped up or disappeared)

· But <u>Moveyhouse</u> was a happening of place (as was <u>Washes</u>, <u>Autobodys</u>)
incidents grew to larger degree out of <u>place</u> in these three, a
fragmentary construction. no theatrical interest

<u>MASSAGE</u>, 1966, Stockholm

* · notationer efter ankomst!

· owned Sw. dumbbells to exercise. black paint w. gold pt. - to

develop body

· cemetery-spaces

· blindfolded and on boat

· TOURISTS

· cemetery-stationery

· typewriter is a way of speaking by sound, hesitations etc.

* · GE MEJ ZEBRAN!

* · "RES MED MEJ STINA....RO MED MEJ TIL CHINA....ARKEN SKA GUNGA....

I EN RODDBÅT....DET GÅR SÅ LAGOM FORT...."

· how do you like the mother-son scene beside you?

* · "TREDJE MAN'S ÅR....JAG SÅG FILMEN SJU GANGER....TRE GÅNGER

SEN...."

· Copenhagen airport sound

* · blindfold + warm korv (I hand)

· things to do on board a boat

· ship's games

· show beard film

· go to "Myrorna"

· LOADING a cow - someone w. many packages

· ROPE

· Shadows - shadowplay

· film projection?

· Everyone gets hats - which are yanked away - hang from ceiling

· Blindfold

- megaphones
* - RÖSTA MJUK   (ÅKE MJUK)
- other words
- GIVE IN
- VOTE SOFT
- VOTE HARD
* - SUCK
* - PRICK
* - FART
* - RUNKRÖKT COPIST ROSTAR DRUVAN

91

- Thunder - film of storm.

- <u>NORDLUND</u>

* - PHYSICAL THEATER FOR PASSENGERS ON BOARD A SHIP.

- deliberately take subject full of symbol + emotion as incident

  + <u>fact</u> only. for my <u>own</u> use as symbol + emotion, having not

  necessarily to do with what I take.

- Nordlund an anti-hero

- Nordlund - no one

Amok är ett malajiskt ord som betyder raseri, ett så våldsamt raseri hos en individ, att denne önskar sin ege undergång — men samtidigt vill ta så många medmänniskor med sig i graven som möjligt.

Ett aktuellt exempel: studenten som spred död och fasa från tornet vid universitetet i Austin, Texas, för några månader sedan.

Vi har i Sverige i modern tid haft två sådana amoklöpare och jag ska i dag berätta om den förste som en majdag 1900 skrev in sitt namn på ett av de mörkaste bladen i vår kriminalhistoria.

Även om många i dag inte finns som kan ha ett direkt minne av mordorgien är det säkert fler som av sina föräldrar hört talas om Johan Filip Nordlund, "Vilddjuret på Prins Carl".

En lång man i blå regnkappa

Medan Österns amoklöpare handlar i blint raseri tycks oftast deras motsvarigheter i Västerlandet psykiskt orka med att tämligen noggrant planera sina dåd. Men inte heller de känner till något om de blivande offren, de slår den som kommer i deras väg.

En annan gemensam egenskap brukar vara, att gärningsmännen i förväg inte visar några tecken på sinnessjukdom. Det kan tvärtom vara vänliga, lugna individer som plötsligt grips av vansinnet.

Ingen på det lilla hotellet i Köping tyckte heller att gästen, "hr Grönqvist", uppförde sig onormalt. Den långe, smale mannen i den mörkblå regnkappan tycktes visserligen inte ha något bestämt ärende i den lilla mälarstaden. Han gick ofta ut på promenader, den 17 maj nedåt hamnen där den vita båten Prins Carl samma kväll skulle avgå till Stockholm.

Befälet tyckte kanske det var litet märkligt med främlingen som flera gånger på dagen gick ombord, tittade in i olika utrym-

- SEARCHLIGHTS

- FILM ON BOAT REVERSE

* - OMBORD VITA BÅTEN

- <u>Å Ä Ö</u>

- Scale is always a corruption thus the performance for sixty people
  is not as corrupt as the performance for 600 or 6000. Popular-
  izers aim at scale and corruption. looseness in order becomes
  disorder
- with people like Lebel, Moorman, Kaprow, Vostell, and Minujin a
  creation of state of disorder for itself or for no clear purpose
  (avant garde) or for political reasons (justified say by amusing
  the populace but actually training them for riots)
- its no surprise that "happenings" of this direction are popular at
  this time
- time of irrevocable dissolution unmanageable dissolution
- * TUB
- SWIFT
- BUT
- * KAR BADKAR BATHINGMAN
- * SKROV VARM SKROV
- BAND TO PLAY
- TUB I
- * POP ANIARA
- OUTWARD BOUND
- * OMBORD (ABOUT TABLES)
- TRIP OUT
- 64 piece for mus was to be bout tables looking up at them as under
  skirts
- TUB
- Composition for an audience on a boat for traveling audience for

an audience of travelers composition for passengers   Cabins

Steward

· MANY ROOMS OF DIFFERENT KINDS   INSTRUCTIONS IN EA FOR PASSENGERS

AND THEN OTHERS (MINE) TO HELP CARRY OUT AND DO OTHER THINGS

· SOMEONE MEETS US   BOARDING OR LANDING

· Lecture room

· film room

· change lights or dim them

· bamboo poles

· Reading about the murderer Nordlund how he researched the ship

where he intended to committ his berserk   I realized   I must do

this too study the ship   tho my intentions are not to murder but

still must know the space completely

· account of a murder   real dramatic act is often the takeoff for a

place and mood for a piece

● En underlig man i lång blå regn-kappa gick ombord på mälarbåten Prins Carl i Köping år 1900. Efter några timmar hade han försökt döda alla ombord.

Mördaren är fortfarande en gåta. Var han sinnessjuk?

· Carl - my name-day

· a friend of Ma's Pa

· her birth date

· Pontus has his triggerfinger, he says.

94

- TUB - TUB (Tube) English - Swedish

- KIT: everyone gets a deck of cards - or newspapers. collaged from all sources. (EAT) (READ) (LOOK AT SIGHTS) (PLAY CARDS)

- ? film daylight

- coming from america perhaps i dont realize enough that words <u>do</u> count pens a sword and that in america words dont count & one can usually say anything one <u>feels</u> like

- noone believes what you say

- is this true

- My experience after doing performances over years since 60 is looking back because i give in to situations i find myself in.

- My performances are a play with nature (nature usually city that is nature with people and made by people who part of what i mean by nature, a play with all that presents itself)

- It would be wrong if any performance in a place under certain conditions would be taken as an imposing on the circumstances or a play in the sense of theater a revolutionary intention or the provocation of change (which I may advocate and further by means outside my performance such as they are or my art)

- I try to provide the container (the one most apt) for the circumstances to develop.

- It is a question of everything of course symbols included but they are not mine. its more like taking a temperature or making an analysis of the local body

95

- People are involved because they are here they are already involved in what is here. I have no desire to change them or tell
  them what to do and certainly not to rescue them in any way and
  very much not to amuse them. Practically speaking they are for me
  like a group of trees.
- <u>Tickets at bridge</u>
- wait in museum.

"DET ÄR
EN GALNING
LÖS OMBORD!"

- Pool - New York
- outdoor Sthlm - real water
- Tub is boat full of water
- Sthlm is water and rocks
- TUB = BED
- sluss - locks
- how long

96

- I mention this because the European idea of the happening is only a sort of bohemian stunt night

- nice title: STUNT NITE

- something like fishing

- i may quit these performances and do something in which i tell how i feel instead of how others feel

* · SILL Y

- Herring X

- studio ive been using at museum musing is good place to film

- one night film pat her musical on such a floor shiny hard sound? her naturally her music her musical

- My performances (this word is more + more ironic) or my "happenings" now consist of choosing a site and container (in this case a ship) and developing the motives found there. Borrowing or renting a piece of nature for a short time and using it for my own purposes. These are both logical and unlogical and often an object is used in a way it was not intended to be used.

- There is no question of the spectators <u>creating</u> the piece (there never has been). They are however at the center of the piece, a part of the scenery. This comes from a recognition that they are as much "objects" as the chairs they sit in. Their thoughts and their feelings may also be considered "objects".

- There may be no way of "seeing" the piece. Only of "being" the piece.

- The reference in the title to the berserk Nordlund who murdered 5 on a Malären boat in 1900 lends the site certain wider possibilities in past time and association and provides for possible use a

certain sequence and structure of events. But this piece is not
in any engaged or particular way about Nordlund or his deed. The
fact involved here is not Nordlunds behavior but an account of the
crime I read recently in Aftonbladet.

- It is never possible to "write" these performances in advance or
before exploring the site or even before the players are brought
in contact with the site.

- The ideas come from the place + things there to accept.

- It is also never possible to experience the full performance until
after the addition of the ingredient of spectators ie. after
1st nite

- Instructions

- The spectators will meet at X for boarding. The trip is expected
to take about an hour with additional time for loading and un-
loading. Bring along crossword puzzle a varm korv (without bread)
a blindfold (the boat is heated)

- Tickets are available only by reservation call X and purchase
tickets at boarding or pick up tickets in adv. at Moderna Museet

* - Nordlund berserk Bear serk björn nalle monument bearboo

*   hjortron

* - mors lilla polar bear positions

- Problem is that few people understand the seriousness of play

- Olle Björn

- <u>rent or buy or get</u>

- V. KORV WAGON (license)

98

- 2 ships - glass top

- from Skeppsholm to Djurgårdsbron (docking there?) 10-10:30

- truck - w. screen

- + Sv. Radio SF sound truck 220V

- portable searchlites

- 200 flashlites

- canteens

- soap + towel

- cars for traffic jam

- torches

- Skeppsholmen permission

- Djurgården permission

- costumes for women.

- Massage-massacre
- * the bears in the museum shocking like Rbergs goat
- SS in midle
- also Mass Age
- A sound piece even the record has to have a conn. in my experience
- * the old folks film used by Öyvind was very effective that hopelessness my only contact w. winter in Sweden
- compulsion not to waste anything
- closet with clothes three interprets: church - organ church - choir woods - lion
- organ - massage bellows
- massage parallels
- sprained ankle plus gold moose plus bicycle rider caught
- Nov. 22 Ann of Kenn Assass. I like identify with him is it then accident that my poster will be life (death) mask on plate with chips out of head (purely physical experience of otherwise horrible event. Kenn.-Nordlund)
- MON. for LONDON (Europe)
- plays a part weather
- tendency to think too fast in terms of real situation relax people
- spectators can stand more than you think they should principle of "more than you think" always in piece
- * clarify adjustment principle (Nissefex)
- the rain did wash away the cheap wine

100

- I am too insesinsitive to local customs
- Using film in this piece is not film of the piece but in the piece clear still and a part of it - thats new
- to imagine what an audience might do is also reality principle exercise (Kaprow used to fail in this) Dewey tells them which is also a sort of failure.
- Suggest make by conditions necessary
- garderoben - biologisk museet
- theme more or less always autoerotism or "playing" with oneself ie. ones mind too
- ear equals manhattan equals oyster
- "do you remember when you used to use real eggs instead of painted ones"
- why is the tape of typing concrete
- aileen's ballet a prefiguration.
- TUBE cornucopia.
- a piece which is set but maybe improved - performed w. changes + add.
- organs cant hit climaxes
- growls = outboard motor (substitute)
- I go around 1st nite rehearsal
- "no beautiful Swedish blond" - Pat says
- sound of my creaky muscles my creaky breathing typewrite - me
- my only exercise - typewriter (soft typewriter equals lung sac)
- The european who have had enough of rules want freedom and the americans who have had enough of freedom want rules even if they

are silly rules (or the rules <u>must</u> be silly) Hence difference
between styles of hapngs. The motivations of the hapg as they are
described and written especially sound absurd. Which is the same
as to say the subjects in sculpture and painting are absurd. The
naming of figures as bears or nurses etc. mean nothing - only the
visual results.

· a convenience of nomenclature

· ghosts or distorted recollections of innumerable conventions now
merely material

· when an artist writes about art his own art I mean he is more
under a responsibility to report the truth but that does not exist
so he feels worse about it than a critic

· a great many attitudes as well things arise from the contact the
city in preparing a piece usually a hostile contact because one
does not get what one wants

· sleep and presence

· gym shoes walks across floor (of big hall)

· In Sweden or in Europe I take myself seriously believe what I
write and feel like a person and not part of a group or machine

· THE Eyes and for that matter all the senses of the body and the
body should be used as much as going to "see" an art show

* · KROPPKAKA

· BODY ELECTRIC

* · I MUSEETS GARDEROBEN OCH ANNANSTANS

· on walls of museum - shadow play

· cloud effects projected.

- mirrors among coats – strong lites reflecting

- sometickled on a bench. TUBE? light projected?

- blindfolds

- searchlights. – use window effects lites thru

- varma korvar i handen. also candy: banana, worms

* - cocobollar

- Linde on vibes. other musicians?

- a Copenhagen sound for gabrielle

* - städning

* - sparkboll. blindfold? not move too much

* - my face tied on – print ALLKOPIA

- badminton falls

- comes down

- attach skirts to bottom

- walk around. just legs ie.= plugs

- + heads only

- arms tied – walks around.

- TUX – doll

- fog machine – smoke (check if anyone else did)

- cigarette smoke in garderob.

- one audience (dumbbell) sees one set. then it is replayed as something else.

- garden furn. – <u>big umbrella</u>

* - hängmatta

- Tent
- * · smell of Klister
- * · ded. TO OSCAR ANDERSON
- · cough record
- * · älskling
- * · "vad gör ni där?" (voice of police) use.
- · RICO-BIG WOOD COSTUME. DRILL
- · FILM how. Electric train
- · audience on bicycles - white cycles
- · tables hanging
- · AMPLIFIERS
- * · TOPLESS - Handelsbanken - or in windows of museum
- · Swing thru air.
- · WHAT HAS GONE BEFORE?
- · discotheque effects film from below use structure
- · giant soft utensils
- · big object cut outs
- · Bells on clothes
- · bamboo rods
- · dance w. household objects - people pull furniture (benches) lying down. clothes attached to furn.
- · project fire into fireplace
- · (does it take a year or two to build up ideas for hapgs.?)
- · sunset
- * · PORR?
- · hammering above - recording of me imitating sawing

- greek fragment

- mailbox. brass

* - MATSAL

- IS HE TRYING TO SAY SOMETHING?

- orchestra

- hanging things

- dresses connected

- big fan

- audience structure they lean forward - are lowered down

- Swing

- running bases

- ripping up clothes

- outboard motor

- heels in c-board. soft music.

- strip (poker)

- Light responsive to breathing

- prick dance. foot cost.

- Opening the window makes the ——— too compulsive - too necessary.

- GIVE THING

* - (GENERAL ELECTRIC) GE - TING

105

- Himself - Conductor - time "Death" - you know (grim Reaper) - Master of Symmetry.

- VARM KORV 2nd nite too hard

- Massage - Masturbate

- Sweden:

  Sleep

  Mechanics

  Sentimentality

  Normality

- everyone normally dressed exc. Pat + me. We try our silly costumes

- Hapg is anti-symbol or anti-meaning or poly-meaning. Therefore asks no point of view of actors or response from audiences but presents them w. loaded or hot material for their use.

- Players are objects. Stress this mechanical quality.

- hence use of convention which corresponds to use of ordinary things in solid work. The meaning lies beyond appearance and name (definition) in a living combination.

- possibilities - often contradictory.

* - The hapg is less theater + more art (konst)

- Golden Moose

- Bicyclist

* - gabrielle - cut-outs skjut + drag..

- soft teeth

- Roll Blankets cut w. knife

- acts must be useless but right

- Bears - garb. bag. twine.

* - "HÅLL NATUREN REN" (label)

- comp

- kitchen help

- Sleep - death

- draw <u>ear</u>

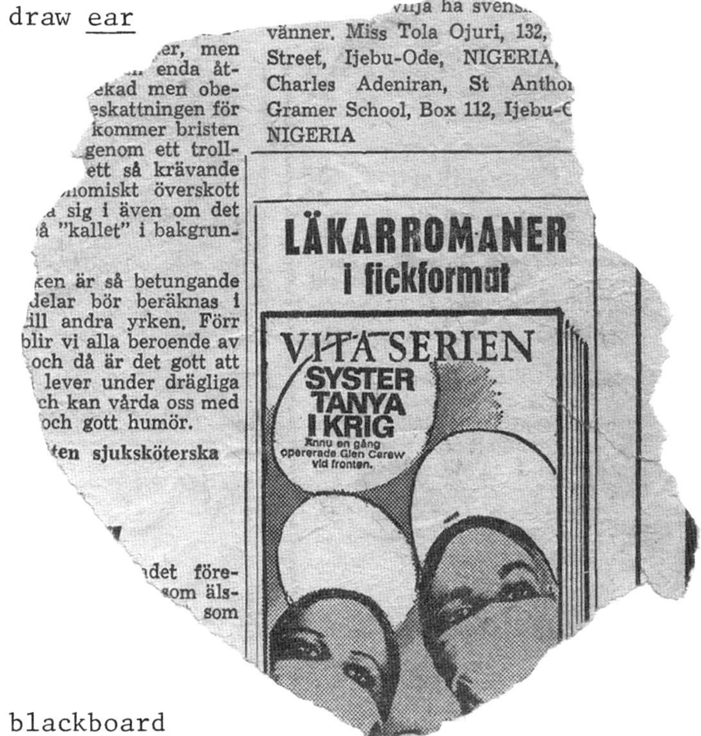

- blackboard

- make bed on stairs up + down

- Pat shake sheets

- undress

- disrobing

- alarm clock

- MORPHEUS

- M = pillow = cig butt = knees

- M = us in bed

107

- FED INTO VENUS
- Modern Mass Massage message
- EM = C
- M^2
- forms of <u>MASS</u> <u>AGE</u>
- suggest implies SADO MASOCH MASOCH
- Peter Lorre
- Mass - religious + scientific + sociological
- Masses
- Massa

* - Masse - works in museum
- "who is the (M) Orpheus Rag Man of my dreams"
- OPERA
- Mickey Massage
- Massage - means same in Sw. + US
- Castle = Cave.
- Relatives title
- things matter = length of time, effect of noise it is 1) con-
  texted (relative) 2) changeable into its opposite (by natural
  law)
- noise = silence
- one is interested in the experience not the repetition. Museum
  version of the experience

* - Syster Mia

* - Olive mon.? L. holmen? make?
- butter

108

* · STAFFAN in piece? help.

  · Big scale of typewriter sound.

  · supposition of being a monster

  · film (falling?)

  · Key out of pants thru hole in pocket

  · film: sculpture in rain

  · spray outboard motor w. hose

  · feather duster

  · vacuum cleaner - Mette or Gabrielle or bears

  · typewriter sound = tape-recorder switches sound

  · surprised by grey tone of hapg. (I would have thot <u>color</u>) or
brown autumnal (but blankets grey)

  · high heels

  · Mette. walk to wardrobe

  · help w. clothes

  · how to tell them. demonstrators.

  · card

  · help - 2 or 3. add there

  · VARM KORV = flashlites

  · TALCUM - MON

  · Ceiling effects

  · museum as temple #2

* · Storkyrkan (like plug)

  · Kinetic art is usually a bore because its path of action is so
limited. Participation art is a bore for the same reason, unless
the situation is very complicated unpredictable. Or human

natural rather than mechanical. The "happening" mechanizes

nature, human action, which is to say sets up more interesting

possibilities than mechanism alone.

- is electronics different from mechanism?

- my monument

- (sign mover)

- pt of view is tragi-comic

- people in daily life accustomed as they are to being symbols
  "dressed up" (but no action occurs) waiting to act their roles.
  This tranferred to theater where ordinarily dream action does
  occur

- hapg – the monument or v.v.

- Bears outside directing traffic

- bamboo – gabrielle MON.

- ropes + dividers

- smoke pot?

- out window. dry ice? MON.

- Matt piska

- new tape under better conditions

- desire to do nite scene. version of day-lite show.

- hospital

- photo gabrielle's place

- in studio shadow play – sound.

- people run up + down stairs, call from door.

- meanwhile the closet action + this comes forward

- clothes + people laid down hoisted like <u>flags</u>

- (audience is <u>lying</u>)

- explosion of some kind - smoke out hole.

- package carried down - it is light balloons or plastic balls but is made to seem heavy - wrapped. placed on sculpture stand Hoisted up as if heavy, then dropped just floats - on ground. It is deflated sent off in a baby carriage

- (Me put into cone roll?)

- Wrap bears in newspaper. they wrap themselves in dance-wrestle

- When people come in chairs are turned toward stairs - after ward-robe piece. chairs are turned around + also seats removed + old clothes placed there

- people camp down all over w. varm korv - flashlites all lites out

- aud. lie down

- big calm

- ssh

- film of screaming tearing noise

- in ceiling??

* - <u>ide</u>

- me wrapped (houdini) put into cone

- film of my ear massaged

- Olle? MASSAGE TUBE or?

- take red out of tube. roll up tube at bedroom wall. work w. Olle.

- 1st nite Olle tube me demonstrate.

- Someone to watch tapes + lites

- FORMS OF MASSAGE

111

- SKY STUFF ADD LATER

- more furs

- mirror ball

*   · news clips on murder

- smell of talc + gas motor

*   · make Picasso sculpt every day.

*   · raise enormous heavy K bröd flag. painted plaster. bears oppose.

- Nisse takes over Pontus

- The Bore

*   · SÖNDAGS-NISSE STRIX

- Xmas hat. S Claus

- + Pontus

- the moose

- vacuum = outb. motor.

*   · NISSE is ANTI - PLUG - pulls them out every nite also GEORGE DENNY

- Finale: Bears throw boxes + take blankets away

- blankets untouched = people who didn't come, graves

- pulley - pats leg. traction

- raise flag finale? bears - tattered silly flag.

- Sound from distance

- water runs

- vacuum cleaner

- toaster pops

- typewriter types

- ping pong game

- blender mixes
- noise (sounds of works)
- lie outside eating Kbröd pick flowers
- rock = blankets
- Bears cued by red spot. light
- on flower rock
- Mouse - picasso
- sandpaper
- MOTIVATE BEAR ACTION ORGANISE
- Brooms
- more noise
- tear cloth
- come out + pretend to sleep
- fish. pole w. ris.
- rip clothes in closet
- run back in toilets.
- 2nd nite good sense of time
- more people laying out blankets?
- blindfolds hard to separate
- <u>scissors</u>
- blanket bus must travel - I pull
- * someone on top like "hölass" cutting rope (retie each day)
- Bears? sit on flower rock w. pathetic mouse Picasso.
- blindfolds - <u>lay out</u> - like cig-girl Mette

113

* · M. M.

* · Komposition för garderob med kappor, trappa, några rum, dörrar,

åskådare,

m. m.

av Claes Oldenburg

(en happening)

Tue Wed Thu Oct 1966

· garderoben

· trappan

* · i stiltje

· ide

· MASSAGE I (in museum)

AV CLAES OLDENBURG

* · 1. Avklädning

· 2. Gymnastik

· 3. Vila (med Dröm)

· FILM

· Claes Oldenburg part in this piece, as Instructor will be filmed

during the period of performances, so that the piece may be

repeated with his image.

· Helpers

* · Pat Oldenburg - pytt i panna

· Mette Prawitz - guide

· Gabrielle Björnstrand - "angel"

114

- Rico Weber - bear I

- Claes Oldenburg - ?

- Olle Granath

- daily made films by Staffan Olzen and Anders Wahlgren

* - 1 tech ass't + 3 helpers   blonde   bl hair girl   SIX MAIX

- The composition takes place in the NW end of the Museum and is

  divided into three parts

* 1. garderob   o   Hylla   avklädning

  2. Ide   gymnastik

* 3. I Stiltje   sängdags

- MASSAGE

  Komposition for Moderna Museet

  in six parts

  lasts about 35 min.

* - med hjälp av

- players + helpers

  István Almay   BEAR

  Gabrielle Björnstrand   PLUG   MUSHROOM

  Olle Granath   MASSEUR

  SIX MAIX BEAR

  Pat Oldenburg   SLEEPER

  Claes Oldenburg   POSTMAN

  Mette Prawitz   NURSE

  Rico Weber   BEAR

  add <u>liers down</u>

115

· SPECTATOR SLEEPERS

· and some who lie down

* · några andra som hjälper till med at lägga sig och åskådarna som

  också lägger sig så småningen.

· MASSAGE (DRIVEIN BATTLEFIELD) MASSACRE

  Komposition for Moderna Museet

  av Claes Oldenburg

  3*, 4, 6 och 7 oktober kl. 21.30 i museet

· Med hjälp av

* Ist007 Almay (Björn) Djur?

* Gabrielle Björnstrand (svamp) Sköterska

* Olle Granath (Massör)

  Six Maix (Björn)

* Pat Oldenburg (Sovande) pytt i panna mon(ument)

* Claes Oldenburg (Brevbärare) Massör

  Mette Prawitz (Sköterska)

  Rico Weber (Björn)

· och några andra som hjälper till med at lägga sig

· och åskådare som också lägger sig så småningom

· Föreställningen varar ungefär 45 min.

* · * generalrepetition

116

- MASSAGE

- ½ hour

- <u>SOUND</u> SOUND OF TWRITER THRUOUT

- Prolog - w. Bears in garden. if no rain. no lite no sound.

- After a wait people come in

- I tell - (Please sit where blankets are located or stand.)

- <u>Claes</u> - The postman - I cue. by handing out addressed letter

- <u>Pat</u> on stand w. balloons, boxes, egg. <u>Spot on her</u>.

- <u>CUE</u> - Exercises, make the bed

- <u>CUE</u> - Sleeps, toss + turn, Balloons break

- SNORE + PHONO (her sound)

- <u>Olle</u> takes tube down from side of bedroom w. ladder.

- <u>Spot</u> on him.

- massages

- <u>CUE</u> - empties + rolls

- (his sound)

- <u>Mette</u> assists the spectators in sitting down on the blanket, ties

  the blind-folds around their eyes + puts them to bed - saying:

  what is in envelope

- <u>Flashlite</u>

- <u>Gabrielle</u> under sack tied to ceiling.

- benches w. bell

- on white bench

- <u>flashlite</u>

- moves about. breaks wood

- pulley

117

- (SOUND)

- bell

- <u>Stefan</u>, <u>Rico</u>, <u>Six</u>

- in toilet run out + go thru clothes.

- <u>Colored lights + switch</u>

- eat bread

- wrap ea other

- (their sound)

- I TURN ON LITE CUE – TO COME OUT

- I GIVE LETTERS CUE – TO END

- <u>THEY END</u>

- go thru audience open doors + epilogue Bears outside. if no rain

- Bears take off cost.

- Outboard.

- Hawaiian music

- record from on Beach at Waikiki

- prolog.

- Coatroom - aud. coats hung up

- Their illumination + sound?

- 1. demonstrating compositions + personality of furniture + bags? + benches + clothes

- ironing board

- Pat is ironing

- <u>aud</u> move chairs receive old clothes

- 2. demonstrating softness + w. sculptures

* - <u>sitt ej i stolarna</u>

- metamorphoses

- undershirt orange pants glasses

- <u>aud</u> pass big ball

- 3. demonstrating sleep sculpture

- <u>aud</u> sleep + turn.

- blindfold, then leave sleep.

- film - of me closeup.

* - SÅ - INTE SÅ

- dont use background.

119

· I. <u>approach + divertissement</u>

· The spectators enter by the side door thru outdoor cafe into long room, past the garden. They pass the bears cavorting with a (body) in the Picasso garden (perhaps a soft picasso sculpture).

* Cardboards resembling P planes or (biolog museum) The Museum is completely dark inside and the front door locked with a sign:

* STÄNGT

· (bears later go in)

· The people walking in create shadow(s) on the facade of (the museum)

· Music + details of waiting.

· II. <u>disrobing + waiting</u>.

· Their coats are taken from them by 2 girls w. hygienic masks Gaby Mette transported by 3 others or more. They can see nothing of what takes place inside.

· III. <u>Tableaux</u>. <u>The Museum church</u>. <u>Mass</u>.

· TAPE WILL CUE

· The spectators are let in. They are guided to (are drawn to) the wardrobe where their coats have been hung up.

· <u>Past the exhibits</u>

· 1. <u>the bears</u> to left

· BEARS wrapping each other in paper + eating kbread

· 2. Pat sleeping pytt-i-panna

· light on curtain

· and 3. Gabrielle w. blackboard drawing line w. long white ruler hooked to ceiling bamboo poles

120

* · Mette w. bicycle TELE + red costume guides them + reveals wardrobe

· MY MOTHER TOLD ME NOT TO PLAY WITH FOOD

· The effect is that of a "church" (the coats are like organ pipes

  or altarlike "choir" or "altar" STRONGLY illuminated IN COLOR.)

· 9 min. up + down

· Widor record from at least two sources

· blankets on floor

· I run up + down stairs w. cord.

· IV. <u>gymnastics</u>

· The organ music slows to stop.

· Growls in wardrobe

· (coats - woods)

· After a while the lights go out in the wardrobe and the curtain is

  pulled shut by the "liontamer" (who stays and will show it later

  during perf turning on growls + lites again) control of lights

· (it looks like a cage)

· A film (or demonstration) which will bring people over goes on at

  opp side from bearroom across on wall over Pat

· typewriter

· or Gabrielle starts to write, lights projector - slips in what?

· SKJUT - DRAG

· Spectators gather between pat-on-sculpt and bears and facing film

  on wall

· NOW blankets are passed out to them

· The film shows how to use blanket

* · Mette shows them (like she shows around museum)

- the tape sound of the typewriter at 1 7/8

- it then shows how to lie down

- it then says please lie down for a long time

- demonstrate FILM SLOW

- (other tape? at same time)

- From time to time draw back curtain at wardrobe and growls from wardrobe

- 2 TIMES?

- bears wrap self in <u>paper</u>

- (difficult section)

- Pat turns in her sleep

- perhaps a balloon breaks (a fart)

- Gabrielle draws on bboard BAMBOO POLE

- at bedroom wall - lighting - OLD PROJ. SLIDE VIEWER

- Other film goes on when people are down

- V. Sleep Rest + dreams <u>Trip</u>

- (? Hawaiian song Kings Serenade at 33)

- Bears emerge w. burlap bags of leaves + "ris" (dreams) + eat K-bread

- Gabrielle walks about (like ghost) passes out blindfolds + varm korv (wagon comes in)

- Olle raises tube + draws out

- RED SAIL RISES

- VI.

- Pat wakes up. some pops then more then more

- Mette + Gabrielle says "wake up"

- WIDOR again

- bears raise plaster flag

- Front door now opens up BRIGHT LIGHT IN coat room opens after church lights how many + which go on We start clean up put sculptures back etc (pick up varm korv)

- As people leave, Varm Korv outside

· MASSAGE

· 1. <u>Approach and Diversion in Sculpture Garden etc.</u>

· The spectators coming to the Museum climb the hill towards the
Museum finding the Museum lights out. It is completely dark inside and there is a sign on the door: STÄNGT.
The floodlight illuminating the right side of the building casts
shadows of the spectators as they are guided around the right side
of the building (past the garden, through the outdoor cafe and
into the Museum by a side door, where they buy tickets and wait).

· waving a sculpt. on rope

· As they pass the Sculpture Garden (Picasso sculptures in concrete)
they see a Biological Museum Tableau: Two Bears who come to life
from time to time and lift (seemingly) the sculptures out of the
ground and break them up. (The "Picasso" which is lifted is made
of grey cardboard, drawn on. Thus the sculptures are returned to
the original cardboard material)

124

- MASSAGE

- II. <u>Disrobing (Avklädning)</u> (and <u>Waiting for the Performance to
  Begin)</u>

- The coats of the spectators are taken by two women wearing
  hygienic masks (like nurses). Passed by them to three helpers who
  take the coats (as if stealing them and with the suggestion of
  uncertainty as to their destination), carry them into the wardrobe. The wardrobe is located in the main room some distance
  away.

- In the wardrobe the helpers hang the coats on "floating" hooks
  (they are so constructed sets of 40 or so on grids attached to
  ceiling) to make a full effect (there will not be enough coats to
  fill the space). Like a forest or an organ or a huge choir. Or
  like hanging coats. (give no checks first night and see if confusion results)

- korv wagon pushed thru

- bears

- strip clothes slowly

- make mess.

125

- MASSAGE

- III. <u>Tableaux</u>: (Mass) <u>Walk to Wardrobe</u>.

- <u>The Typewriter</u>

  The spectators are admitted to the main room from the entrance at
  the opposite end of the long room. Up to this time this door has
  been shut. (They have been handing over their wraps through the
  counter at the door into the Museum collection room) They are
  <u>guided</u> to the Wardrobe past the Exhibits by Mette who wheels a
  TELE orange bicycle, straddling it from time to time or turning it
  upside down. She wears a red costume (athlete top and boxer
  trunks and white stockings?) and hygienic mask. (mask only) She
  says repeatedly: "My mother told me never to play with food."
  (Later, when gives korv) Reaching the Wardrobe which is covered by
  a curtain, she puts down the bike (stands it upside down?). Pulls
  the curtain aside as if revealing a monument, revealing the
  "stolen" coats hung. This scene is brightly illuminated in pink
  and blue and yellow lights (red) (wardrobe is open – coats there)

- Typewriter sound

- (Music: Widor organ Toccata has been playing since beginning
  of III.)

- Is there a sign reading: "Though the objects invite touching we
  ask you not to..." (the Swedish sign at my exhibit)

- They sit down on blankets

- tells what they are for

- Mette remains here showing the Wardrobe until after the Toccata
  ends and through the following passage of Lion Roars. At the end

of the Lion Roars she closes curtain again.

- (She opens the curtain 3 minutes about later when the roars return, and so on. The roars return at 3 minute intervals through the sound of the Typewriter (which begins after the end of the first set of roars).
- Bears
- Six helps. as bear
- blow horns
- break stix
- pails kick
- Mette is on the main floor when the Lion Roars are not on, helping with the Gymnastics (Blankets and Varm Korv) and Tucking People In and then helping them to Wake. (Without her bicycle).
- The Exhibits which the spectators pass on their way to the Wardrobe are the following:
- See:
- 1) 200 folded <u>Army</u> blankets with newspapers (blindfolds) and a warm sausage on them (exercise devices) (like cemetery) neatly placed in rows (like knäckebröd).
- 2) Olle, in white rubber overalls with (how) (lowers slowly) a giant 400 cm long toothpaste tube hung from the ceiling rafters (make industrial)
- Floyd Patterson
- pushes massages
- 3) Two "Bears in an enclosure eating knäckebröd and wrapping one another in newspaper with twine.

127

- 4) Gabrielle, in front of the light from an old slide projector
(in which are stencils of letters?) (what represent) at a blackboard, drawing lines with chalk and the aid of a white ruler. On
the lines she writes SKJUT OCH DRAG over and over (drinks milk).
She wears a hygienic mask, a blue nurses costume with headdress.
To her fore arms (near elbows) are attached (hang) long
bamboo poles which reach to an attachment on the rafters of the
ceiling (?)

- 5) Claes (as Nisse) - a busy man. (I Play Nisse) running up and
down the stairs to the "Hyllan" in gym shoes tracing his path
with bright orange string back and forth back and forth (too
tiring?).

- 6) Pat as Pytt-i-Panna in a brown pajamas to which "white boiled
potatoes" are attached, on a bed of pillows of thin muslin stuffed
with blown up blue balloons, covered with a giant fried egg.
(+ boxes).

- phono.

- gradually build up.

- music with it

- model stand

- shake egg

- Talcum

- Time: Widor 16 min. max. Lion about 4 min. Total: 20 min.

- Lights: Small light over Pat, Projector at Gabrielle

- Sound: Widor Toccata and Lion Roars

128

- MASSAGE

- IV. <u>Gymnastics</u>

  Cue to the beginning of this section is the beginning of the sound
  of the typewriter (at 1 7/8). Cue for the beginning of the typewriter is the end of the Lion Growls in the Wardrobe. Claes or
  another operator turns on the Typewriter tape on Machine no. 2.
  which is located in the main hall against inside wall. Simultaneously a projection begins of a film in which Claes <u>demonstrates</u>
  the use of the blanket and warm <u>sausage and newspaper found for</u>
  <u>the use of the audience at this time.</u>

- The audience is drawn by the film showing away from the Wardrobe
  which is closing and should occupy an area in the center about of
  the main hall.

- Mette instructs as well how to use the blankets etc.

- yes - to lie down

- w. talcum on table

- Olle massages tube

- Gabrielle grabs bamboo poles exercises breaks wood

- meanwhile the action of the others at their stations (continues as
  described) and with additions (plot). Pat turns in her sleep
  popping a balloon or two.

- Time: About 15 min. of typewriter. At 3 min. periods, 3 min. of
  Lion Growls.

- Sound: Tape of Typewriter. Tape of Lion Growls

- (A supplementing tape machine may be out of synch with the others
  to enrich the sound.)

129

- MASSAGE

- V. <u>Rest</u>

- The instruction film ends by me wrapping the blanket around me
  and lying down. (On Mon. I will do the instructions in person)
  The people are helped to do so until as many as possible <u>are</u>
  <u>bedded down</u>. When the typewriter tape ends, the Hawaiian tape
  begins. This is the cue for people to be helped to lie down.

- The audience is supplied with blindfolds

- Mette says: Sleep now

- Mette give varm korv

- "My Mother said never play w. food"

- While the spectators are blindfolded and tucked in and the
  Hawaiian music plays, the Bears emerge eating knäckebröd, carrying
  "ris" such as used by streetcleaners and carrying burlap bags of
  autumn leaves (stenciled LÖV), which they place about.

- too passive

- screaming + beating the people w. branches.

- Olle raises (rolls up) the giant tube and draws from it long red
  (white) tube (?)

- At this time if the spectators are lying, another film may be
  shown perpendicular to the instruction film the length of the main
  hall on the back of the Bedroom Room wall.

- Time: Hawaiian music 13 min.

130

- MASSAGE

- VI. (<u>End</u>)

- Widor Toccata after Hawaiian Music.

- Mette says "Wake Up!" Opens the Wardrobe closet.

- The Front Doors opened by the Bears. A <u>bright</u> red <u>light</u> shines

  in. The Bears go outside to raise a flag dipped in plaster.

- Hawaiian Paradise

- aloha oe

- 4. (picassos)

- We pick up, leaves, bits of sausage etc.

- Put sculptures back

- Lights: Outside a bright light

- Sound: Widor Toccata indefinitely

- PAT

- <u>1st light</u>

- stand is lit.

*
- I approach it via a small stool, carrying one box. Lie down, box on stomach. Move across stand, balancing box first on legs then feet. Do a short action with box in air above head, move it slowly into position on stand, change it from time to time. Leave stand, return with balloon pillow, hold that to catch light, place near box. Bring in mattress, hold above head and move in light. Take a long time positioning it on stand. Return with tennis balls (or small ropes or twigs). Bring in second pillow,
*
  repeat dance action. Bring in bolster (RA). Now come in with large egg coverlet and lie down slowly on balloons, trying not to fall off stage and keeping covered with egg. Balloons break - I help with fingernails and pins Do series of fixing up bed. Break more balloons. Uncover my egg. Toss, turn. change position.

- <u>2nd light</u>

- Bring up T.V. Turn it on. lie motionless for a long time, staring at it, jiggling the knob. Change my position, lie on back, feet against wall, still looking. Change again - on stomach. Get restless - cover, uncover. try by squinting. Turn it off.

- <u>3rd light</u>

- Take book and flashlight - sit up against wall, read with flash. Lie down on balloon pillow under cover, hold book at arm's-length, sometimes moving flashlight over pages, other times moving book

and keeping light stationary. Lie on stomach, arm hanging over
edge of stand with book. Change again several times, restless.
* Try to sleep. Hang up "Ear" and sleep a bit. Wake up, read more,
under the covers, and then doze off when the piece ends.

- METTE Nurse I, and others II III...
- Mask, White the kind nurses' wear hygienic mask
- knife - (miniature hunting) on string around neck. (photo)
- sunglasses on string around neck.
- flashlight with 3 settings: White, Green and Red, for parts I, II
  III. resp.
- black costume -
- TO SAY: MY MOTHER TOLD ME ONE SHOULD NEVER PLAY WITH FOOD (IN
  SWEDISH)
- get bears
- demonstrate
- talk
* - "SOM EN INDIAN"
* - "VAR SNÄLL OCH LÄGG..."
* - "MIN MAMMA..."
* - "OM NI LÅG SA FICK NI V.K..."
- give out varm korv
- do not tell to lie down right away
- gently suggest.

133

- OLLE: Masseur

- costume: white pants, white undershirt

- props: giant tube, table

- lights: spot above, weak light, taped flashlite

- <u>part one</u> (20 min.)

- SOUND 0 / TYPEWRITER 3 3/4 speed

- LIGHT:

  1) SPOTLITE OVER TABLE, LONG WALL

  2) WEAK BULB OVER TABLE HUNG FROM CEILING

- Enter pushing + drawing blanket bus, removing blankets (Bears, under tube, resist)

- When bus is even w. table, remove tube, carry over head (like sculpture of man w. bird) lay out on table.

- straighten, lift. change position etc.

- Return to help unload blankets

- alternate between positioning tube, shaking it etc. and helping lay out blankets.

- <u>part two</u> (15 min.)

- SOUND: 0 / TYPEWRITER 1 7/8 speed

- LIGHT:

  1) SPOT OUT

  2) WEAK BULB REMAINS ON.

- Olle devotes himself entirely to tube. Massaging it, shifting it around and beating it.

- takes out insides – white + red tubes of cloth and ties them up (ready to hoist) ends by rolling up tube and tying it.

- finally lying down next to it.

- <u>part three</u> (10 min.)
- SOUND: O/ TYPEWRITER SILENT
- LIGHT:
- 1) SPOT <u>OUT</u>
- 2) WB <u>OUT</u>
- 3) USE FLASHLITE
- Olle lies by tube w. flash. (exercising slowly with rubber stretcher)
- at end arises and hauls up tube + contents (red + white tubes) in ceiling
- SOUND:
- 1) OUTBOARD M. STARTING
- 2) HAWAIIAN.
- LIGHT: HOUSE LIGHTS

- GABRIELLE: (Instructress):
- <u>Costume</u> = (muse) mask, knife
- <u>props</u> – blackboard w. chalk, sponge + folding ruler painted white
- (megaphone)
- (flashbulbs)
- (vacuum)
- <u>Lights</u> against far wall spot above + small swedish wall lamp
- white benches placed so:
- (w. branches. + sheets)

- part one (20 min.)

- SOUND: 0

- LIGHT:

  1) SPOTLITE OVER BLACKBOARD

  2) WALL LAMP ON.

- Enters w. audience and helps Mette + Six lay down blankets,

  blindfolds, and korv on napkins.

- demonstrates lying down.

- part two (15 min.)

- LIGHT:

  1) SPOT OUT

  2) WALL LAMP ON

  3) (flashbulbs)

- Gabrielle sleeps. first on one bench, then on other – w. blanket

  (or sheet) (branches) (w. vacuum)

- (uses megaphone – says "skjut", "drag")

- (reads papers)

- (rings bell)

- part three (10 min.)

- LIGHT:

  WALL LAMP ON

- Gabrielle wakes up. washes blackboard writes on it "skjut",

  "drag"

- ladle milk.

136

- SIX: (food dispenser)
- COSTUME: WORK-GLOVES, KNIFE
- PROPS CART W. LITE ON WHICH VARM KORV, PAPERTOWEL, TIRE PUMP + TIRE
- LIGHTS: FLASHLITE W. 35 TOPS. CARTLITE
- <u>part one</u> (20 min.)
- THINGS TO SAY (IN ENGLISH)
- also demonstrate how to sleep.
- halfway thru enter w. V.K. from?
- dispense + also inflate tires w. pump.
- Six sausage dispenser
- 1) dolly
- 2) a stainless steel pot of hot sausages "varm korv"
  (100 at least each night)
- 3) towels
- 4) clamps
- 5) rubber mitts (photo)
- 6) flashlight.
- lay out V-K - how
- bullets
- roll - towel

- RICO, STEFAN: (Bears)
- costume: rented "monkey" no mask
- props: Knäckebröd (sandbags)
- LIGHTS: wardrobe lit by blinking colored lites red spots

- <u>part one</u> (20 min.)
- PROLOGUE: ½ hr.: take positions on rock + flowers by restaurant if one asks say: "we are not bears" or "this is the biological museum." (pile sandbags)
- SOUND: (horns)
- LIGHT: WARDROBE. FLASHBULBS..
- Bears enter Museum and take place on blanket bus under tube. Tube is removed + blankets taken off. bears interfere.
- They interfere also w. demonstrators waking them and do themselves parody demonstrations - all around room (they are active)
- at end, when truck gets to end of its course they leap off and go into wardrobe...
- <u>part two</u> (15 min.)
- SOUND: glass break   HORNS
- LIGHT: wardrobe flashbulbs.
- They go into wardrobe
- They push brooms thru wardrobe
- (they fight + tie ea. other w. newspaper + string)
- about half way thru they break glass
- they hammer
- they tear cardboard
- throw boxes
- a little lite?
- <u>part three</u> (10 min.)
- SOUND: CLOTH TEAR
- LIGHT: wardrobe - blinkers no flashbulbs

- tear cloth. sitting in front of stairs. Make a flag by tearing cloth tying it together.
- (they + Gabrielle center of attention = Pat + Olle sleep)
- SOUND: HAWAIIAN
- LIGHT: HOUSE
- bears haul up flag. and walk out.

- LIST OF PROPS and Material FOR MASSAGE
- photos - leave to be photoed (marked w. asterisk)
- <u>claes</u>
- black soft hat*
- white gym shoes*
- trousers (swedish)*
- loose brown sweater*
- open collared white shirt*
- <u>Pat - Sleeper</u>
- spotlight
- bed lamp*
- book to read ("LUXURY MODEL")
- large, pink ear (of cardboard)*
- tiny flashlight
- a number of blue balloons blown up inside muslin: 2 pillows, 1 bolster, 1 mattress
- six white tennis balls
- 1 sealed medium size cardboard box.*
- several very dry tree branches

- pedestal, large as a bed, about 4 ft. high.

- pins

- white underwear*

- brown two piece men's pajamas*

- coverlet sewn in shape of a fried egg + stuffed w. styrofoam "pills"*

- Olle MASSEUR

- large orange and white "tube"*

- two "squeezings", 1 white, 1 red - stuffed cloth tubes.

- long table

- white sheets

- small overhead naked bulb.

- stand (to tie lines to)

- spotlight (white)

- talcum powder

- orange inner tubes

- hand pump

- stick (for beating)

- pulley + line

- flashlight (taped over)

- costume of white undershirt and white jeans (or pants)

- Gabrielle MOON

- a collection of large branches w. many leaves - rather dry

- "lampette" attached to wall (or other lamp)*

- white bed-sheets

- newspapers

- blackboard that flips over.
- sponge*
- water*
- chalk*
- folding ruler*
- 3 white wooden benches*
- spotlight
- gym. 'horse' (ladder)
- sparkboll
- slide projector:

  1) with plastic cap – diffuse light

  2) without plastic cap – strong light, clear frame
- costume? black tights and blackish top costume
- <u>Stefan</u> <u>Rico</u> (Bears)
- two hammers
- sheet of glass (for breaking) + metal container to break it in
- blinking lights of different colors.
- two miniature hunting knives*
- brooms (2)
- colored rags (to tear to make flag)*
- garbage bags (60) of brown paper "Håll Naturen Ren" (Keep

  nature clean) printed on them
- pulley + live
- red spotlight
- 2 "bear" costumes (without heads) rented from Karl Gerhard,

  Sthlm, Sept.-Oct. 1966

- supply of Knäckebröd*

- boat horns (to be carried + used <u>inside</u> costume)

- <u>General</u>

- 200 grey or brown army-type blankets folded into rectangles and tied in bundles.

- cart, on which the blankets are piled*

- outboard motor, in a barrel of water*

- 200 white muslin blindfolds, folded into squares, carried in a box-tray ("cigarette-girl" style).

- tape recorder

- amplifier

- phonograph

- tape: of me composing my notes to the sthlm catalogue on a typewriter Aug. 1966

- Phono record: Hawaiian melodies (33 1/3 rpm)

142

- <u>Pat</u>
- branches
- big boxes
- exercises before bed
- snoring
- <u>Olle</u>
- no costume or undershirt + pants:
- Talcum Talcs his hands
- Table for Tube
- gradually uncovers
- contents
- newspapers.
- <u>Gaby</u>
- milk + ladle
- Megaphone - horn
- program - flash bulb
- Shout: skjut
- go over benches
- Split bags + sew together or muslin
- mushroom
- plug
- enclosure
- wood to break
- crouch
- bench
- dress 38.

143

*   · <u>FILM</u>

   · Pat + me + others

   · drunk   (Me)

   · self portrait

   · <u>SOUVENIR</u>   STHLM 1966

   · KROPP KAKA

   · BODY PROJECTED

   · drop cake – sculpture

*   · lösnäsa

   · soft hammer – carve from foam

   · or plaster

   · HAMMER BREAKS

   · wrestle w. shower   <u>IN TUB</u>

   · just an uncut collection of things

   · mounted + unmounted

   · pressing buttons?   tits etc.?   street, lights, elevator

   · hats

   · Pat + I wrestle in leaves

   · eat kbröd

*   · try to pass on left   left – right on bro

   · step in shit

   · fall in sidewalk ruts

*   · try cross Nybroplan

   · feel things up – little shots – statues

   · (MA   SS / AGE – <u>write things</u>)

   · two figs.   Pat + me + blanket + pillows.   cut out.   move. of paper

- fan

- small lamp buy   just burns

* - <u>smiles</u> - Mynt munnar

- bread eaten + drops pick it up eat it   smaller + smaller

- cut nails.

- end w all asleep

- film w. v. korv

- <u>Mon</u>

    1. face dissolve

    2. me wash

    3. walk in studio   shoes

    4. studio

    5. iron Knäckebröd falling

- <u>Wed</u>

    1. Mask in box

    2. "   out of cooler + on tray

    3. coke bottles

    4. eating + drinking   Kbröd + liver saus

    5. neck swallowing

    6. Parts of face

    7. Tearing cardboard - face appears

    8. typewriter from behind + below

- <u>CONTENTS</u>

  cover

  Introduction - Ulf

  Quotes from me (more or less as captions)

  inventory

  script

  photos

  drawings and report of script pages

  appendix on false starts
- Effect - a small book of poetry in illustrations and words

- A situation should be so clearly prepared (by me) that improvisation will naturally fall within the effect wanted.
- The composition was made in action, including the time of performance with an "audience".
- The "audience" of the first three performances helped define but did not experience the most complete solution of the 4th and final performance.
- in the happening a performance is not complete on "opening night". The steps by which it becomes complete - erasures and additions and adjustments, including false steps - are part of the effect.
- The performance is process - ingenuity and luck, in diminishing time. With the last performance, time's up.
- The particular conditions which shaped the piece will never return.
- Actions are visually clear but ambiguous in meaning. It is the

world without words, or actions seen through a telescope.

- Because <u>everything matters</u>, the performances are not only something experienced collectively by a large group. What matters may be something that happens secretly between two people during the preparation of the piece. A happening for the participant is the whole of his experience - events trivial and important - in and out of the happening locale - within the period of preparation and performance. Perhaps <u>all</u> happening events are trivial.

- After the intention of doing a piece is formally declared (as by mailing out a title, a place etc.), anything that happens is considered relevant. This includes events on a large scale, things one reads about in the newspapers.

- Noone plays roles. The players execute actions, follow instructions. Not only are they not playing roles, they are also not playing themselves. They are agents, machines. There is a style to the performance - a poise, an indifference to anything but what belongs to the execution of the act assigned to a player.

- I am also anatomizing the work of art. I know that a work of art is a complex of motives. When I am through with a piece, I have accounted for and included as many as I could. The art object ought to be a highly concentrated mass, capable of endless reactions.

- With my constructions outside happenings, as in an exhibition, this is not always obvious, or one motive seems more important than others. In the performances, I autopsy both myself and the work of art. The "spectators" are both in the "gallery" and in

the work. In the performances (or demonstrations) I am also both inside and outside.

- The performance is a complement to or extension of the other work.
- In "Massage", the players demonstrated the surfaces and insides of the works on display. There were signs placed by the Museum all around asking spectators not to touch the objects "although the objects invited touching". The demonstrators played hands. They worked on substitutes and similar material and objects – the actual pieces in the show were not used.
- The spectators _imitated_ the works of art, by blindfolding themselves, wrapping themselves in blankets, and obeying the force of gravity.
- The exposure to audience – the "formal" presentation, with tickets sold, is simply the introduction of the physical factor "audience". The performance is not _for_ the audience. They are part of it and shape it. They are not there to look at something but to be part of the landscape – to be looked at or to be used.
- When the audience comes in expecting to sit down and look at something, they are less interesting than when they enter not knowing where or what the action will be, gradually responding to existing circumstances.
- If the audience at the end applauds, it is a sign that the enveloping and non-climactic effect has not been achieved.
- There is no way for me to force a performance. It only becomes what it wants to become by its own making and its own time. There is usually an unsolved part when the "formal" presentation

begins. The situation at the SE end (Gabrielle and her lyrical surroundings) resisted until the final performance. Every day I added or substituted props and changed the position and action. Gabrielle had to put up with the uncertainty. One night she lay down on a bench and fell asleep. During the final performance I saw how it would work out and cued and instructed her (during performance).

· Massage grows out of the two months I have spent in the Museum preparing my show, most of it in the part of the Museum where the piece takes place. Hyllan served as my studio and I ran up and down the stairs many times and into the door to the office. Like all my theater pieces this can not be repeated any more than the experience itself. But if anyone is tempted to try I have written a "ghost" role for myself, so that I will seem to be here even if i am not

· Everything depends on the actual situation. So it is not possible to plan a piece in advance of experience of a place, certain people and other materials and conditions.

· I know this but I cant resist planning things in advance, and it is not easy for me to leave my studio or the room where I am planning and make contact with the facts. I make plans at a distance, before I am actually in the place where the performance will be done. If I am going to a place I have never been, I set down a lot of prejudice and hearsay.

· Once in the place, I make false grasps of the situation and unreal plans at first (although stimulated by facts of the situation.)

149

There is a period of indulgence in whims. These false plans have their importance, and I follow them seriously to impossible conclusions. Many of these false starts are carried into a piece, by the principle of metamorphosis. One must be thrifty and practical. If one has something good, but impractical, something loaded, one can retain it by changing it - the basic form and a lot of the meaning remains, though the occasional shape and context is different. Sometimes the difference, or disguise, is what makes the incident effective. Every idea must be visible and practically realizable. This is where the poetry of this theater is unique. A poet is not limited by what he can actually present - especially under these limited circumstances. (I prefer them so)

· A herd of elephants might be transported into a caravan of marbles. A large part of a performance is hidden in this way.

· The "Strange Mickey Mouse" was originally the sketch of a building to house my museum of popular objects. Used on the letterhead of the correspondence for the Stockholm show, it became a symbol of the Moderna Museet: Mouse; Mus; Muse; Musee

· MM

· Modern Mouse; Modern Muse; Musee Mousse

· In MM's sleepy eyes (half drawn shades) is the theme of sleep (which Ulf Linde later discovered in the show).

· Mickey Morpheus

· In Provincetown, Mass., I once killed a mouse, not intending to. Intending in fact to save the mouse, which my cat had wounded, I

knocked it down a drainpipe beyond reach, where it no doubt died

painfully. I made the following drawing about that time:

$\frac{M}{W}$ (mirror reflection of a mountain)

- Body in bed - Mass

- Mass.

- "MASSE", (name of an employee of the museum)

- Mass (Church)

- Masses

- Massacre

- (Einstein Peter Lorre Marilyn Monroe)

- Masoch

- Modern Mass

- Modern Massacre

- Modern Masseum

- Modern Massage (Mass Age)

151

· MASSAGE

· Massage is associated with Sweden - "Swedish Massage". The word
is spelled the same and means the same in English. In both lan-
guages it carries sexual suggestions. It seemed to mean both what
one ought to wish to do with my work (my body) and what I ought
to wish to do with my audience's body. Communication by touch.

· Though this word was just then associated with McLuhan, I felt my
response personal enough to accept it as the title and the cards
were printed. The title is a decision of great importance. In
searching for a title (it can keep me up several nights) I dis-
cover what I have on my mind, and this sets the general pattern of
thought for the performance.

· The players are given actions to perform that imitate or represent
sometimes metamorphically the actions of their "real" professions
or activities. For some reason, staying in bed became a more important activity in Stockholm than anywhere else. Many variations
of lying and staying in bed developed. I came to think of the bed
as a dance floor, theater, and pedestal for sculpture. Pat's part
in the piece, as a "live" bed sculpture, was a result of this.

· In past performances, I have 1) put myself inside an object,
hidden from view; 2) played a "role" in the piece; 3) remained
indifferent, hidden outside the piece or posing as a spectator.
I have often been tempted to just walk away, take a cab to the
other end of town but I have never done so.

· In Massage, it was not clear to me what my part would be. The

role of "postman" - delivering written instructions in envelopes
for the players to open - proved impractical. Circumstances created the following (as if I had been surprised on stage by the
rising curtain):

· 1) <u>Stage-hand</u>. Laying out blankets, cutting bundles etc. This
developed into:

· 2) <u>Keeper or Determiner of Tempo</u> - "conductor" My pace of laying
out blankets, and later my pace of walking about among the lying
spectators, controlling tempo by the sound of my rubber shoes.
The gym floor was especially resilient and squeaky.

· 3) <u>Overseer</u> or seer-over. I saw the whole from the inside and
outside and was probably the only one bent on seeing the whole.
Moving about and taking vantage points became a kind of "role" -
the "painter" studying the material, raw and shaped. Constantly,
restlessly.

· 4) <u>Demonstrator</u>. I demonstrated behavior for the audience (as did
the nurses), by showing how they should wrap themselves in the
blanket, put on the blindfold, lie down, get up, replace blanket
etc. While "demonstrating" ie. with my blindfold on and
"sleeping" I was aware of being extremely vulnerable. Suppose
someone wanted to express physically how little they cared for
the noise, the inconvenience and my objectives generally? - here
was their opportunity!

· 5) <u>Composer</u>. Organizing the piece, making changes, inventing and
cuing, during performance. Especially deciding duration of
effects, sensing the endurance of a particular audience. For some

long was longer. As a rule I always wait some time beyond what I
consider excruciating because I am inclined to be impatient. Up
to a point extension or repetition in a piece is boredom but there
is a point of breakthrough into a new state of experience. For
example, the "noise" for me finally became silence – the body had
erected its defenses. I have never before heard such silence.

· 6) <u>Symbol</u>. I couldnt restrain my fantasy as I walked about and I
felt myself a symbol of process (time) constantly laying out fresh
material ("bodies", "souls") and also fresh "graves". At times,
the battlefield metaphor (which was not as consciously intended as
it appeared to be) became embarrassingly direct, unambiguous.

THE TYPEWRITER, 1968, New York

155

- I have been asked by <u>Esquire</u> to do an anatomy, an "archaeology" of the happening, in my style, as I once did it. I will make this analysis and produce a description of method with illustrations, and a sample scenario of a piece which may or may not be performed, to be called "The Office" - consistent with the analytical theme of the enterprise.

- The illustrations will consist of 1) literary and graphic materials executed and selected by me, and 2) photos, not by me, of props, costumes, and sample situations using models (in my studio and outside my studio), and of myself at work, using and developing these materials.

- There may be a performance of this piece later, but due to lack of time it cannot be now. <u>Esquire</u> is under no obligation to produce the happening. That the piece cannot be produced at this time doesnt trouble me - it will feed into other work.

- For this demonstration, I will require $1000.00 for materials and salaries; and a fee for my time of $2000.00, including expenses.

- Graphics and writing made by me for the project will remain my property.

- I guarantee the material will not be published before the date of publication in <u>Esquire</u>. I will retain reproduction rights after publication in <u>Esquire</u>.

- Hey this is the hollow table (for erection)

156

- Tuesday December 10. 225 lbs.

- Esquire, to discuss happening possibility. Propose office as
subject.... work until 3 or so on some beginnings, rather
hysterical...DATA as title, etc. Smoke rises through floor from
Chamberlain's film showing....

- Thursday December 12. 225 lbs.

- Inspect data center on Madison Ave., then to Granada TV, 161 W.54,
examine office and approve. Fire next door, door broken in, man
died...

- Mention interest in office sounds, data PR man says they are trying to eliminate them. Many wires run into the floor. Visit sub-
basement full of obsolete processing machines. But space wont do.

- Flaming cemetery dream

- Friday December 13. 225 lbs.

- To office at 161 54th St....Unpack my green bag and make some
calls. Experience the new neighborhood....

- Work in office, make tape, write and read, sun goes down...Walk
into business night..

- First period - expansion....Happening is a diversion of function,
a slowing down of things for analysis. The playhouse of the
natural world.

- Aural emphasis. Muzak. A restaurant - things come out of a hole.
This is/This is not a happening. Absolute darkness, absolute
silence.

- Sunday December 15. 220 lbs.

- Wonderful wakeup in bright snowscene allaround...Write in studio
formulating hapng...

157

- Machine order and repetition, repeated rectangles – search for a subject having repeated rectangles: hospital, school, cemetery, office, morgue. Secretaries, teachers, nurses. The bunks in an Armory.

- Squander money. Who will be the audience now?

- A lecturelike piece?

- In my office I dont know which fantasy to indulge, that of the Private Eye or Analyst.

- Typical perverse: faced with a piece to be photographed I prescribe darkness (outer space) and sound (music of the spheres).

- <u>Monday December 16</u>.   217 lbs.

- <u>Tuesday December 17</u>.   220 lbs.

- Arrangements made for me to occupy a cubicle in the H. Publishing Co., and I do so, arriving 1:30. First day at the office. A tiny room, just for one. I sign a card for a man who has just cleaned the typewriter. I listen mostly – the cubicle catches the sound like a big ear. I get a coffee sample. I hear jokes told, heels. I dial 9. It is the day of the office party, to be held in the Baroque room of the Belmont Plaza.

- B.C., my "secretary" visits and we discuss anti-office events, sounds one would <u>not</u> hear in an office, snoring f. ex. Activity of no direction in the midst of directed activity.

- Was invited to the office party but did not go.

- <u>Wednesday December 18</u>.   221 lbs.

- Granada shows films of cities at war.

158

- People covered with blankets in the shelters - in the office.

- Watching symbols, apparitions, Christ the fan. Combine religious and mundane, "double" objects.

- The White Fleet of muse/secretaries (all black).

- Midtown <u>needs</u> its soft music.

- <u>Thursday December 19</u>. 219 lbs.

- <u>Friday December 20</u>. 220 lbs.

- Pat's leg bruised from falling off chair night before. Cab her to Beth Israel.... T. appears at Granada out of breath - "I ran" "What did you run from?" "I ran from that fucking office!"

- Office party at the Cheetah. Later babbling about return to the body, using <u>Web and the Rock</u> p.? for text.

- Word equals turd. Dynamite blasts around the office.

- Phone is a sphincter - cutoff. Hot line. Umbilical cord.

- A secretary delivers a phone from under the skirt.

- Mother equals phone. Office equals bathroom.

- A big hand to reach down and crush the boss's cubicle, like King Kong.

- <u>Saturday December 21</u>. 220 lbs.

- Make repeated aggressive calls to "directory assistance" which cannot find my number

- Orifice and Eurydice.

- <u>Sunday December 22</u>. 221 lbs.

- Chilled, feverish - sick finally, dying of office parties.

- Lie rigid, hands on stomach, under a blanket, wearing plastic ear covers for two hours.

159

- Monday December 23. 221 lbs.

- In bed, early A.M., scribble first scenario.

  Loudspeakers announce "this is a police situation!" and the

  audience is tied to chairs. Each desk is a stage. Floor of the

  aisles is kept wet.

- In the end everyone is covered with sheets.

- Secretaries spill ink on themselves. Intercom. Hobbled in

  some way.

- Tuesday December 24. 221 lbs.

- Sit under a desk and open drawers upside down. Recall the big

  bubbles in an old water cooler. Film this.

- Where did I file little vignette about shitting into a typewriter?

- Get a stationery catalogue, or take $500.00 and squander it in a

  stationery store.

- Contents of a desk-drawer.

- Cross-breeding of sex and office, body and machine. Masochist

  fantasy: Modern Times. Rubber band - bondage.

- Wednesday December 25. 220 lbs.

- Became aware that Chamberlain's radio had been on for three days

  and nights at the same volume, and imagined I smelled gas or a

  corpse. Supersensitivity to the sound of it.

- Thursday December 26. 219 lbs.

- Create a false "office" in my studio. Devise absurd "office"

  activities, such as copying office sounds over and over in

  different ways.

- Build "stage" for secretary, and isolate typical activities to be

observed, f. ex. use (for my purposes) of a desk lamp or pencil
sharpener.

· Secretary equals artist's model.

· Recall the incident of Ed Kienholz axing the clerk's metal desk
at the L.A. Airport in retaliation for the destruction of his
Tiffany lamp in cargo.

· Chopping up of the manger. Christ is mixed up in here somewhere.

· Destruction of the boss's "soft" office.

· Bendings over, kneelings. Career advice. Shorthand.

· <u>Friday December 27</u>. 219 lbs.

· Due to lack of time, the development is telescoped. Efforts to
convert the material to the flat, silent medium of a photograph
or type on page.

· Mary – Secretary – Secret Mary. Visit model studios with Jim
looking for Secretary.

· Recall movie made of myself long ago in which I destroyed my
"office".

· "Man is the first data processor".

· Billy Klüver: "Information is a limp prick."

· Two parodies come to mind: Courbet – the whole office staff
gathered in his "Studio", and Rodin, who filled his "office"
with nude models going about ordinary business, until he re-
required an 'expressive' pose or two.

· All art, and office, is about indifference to the woman.

· What was the Anouilh play in which the madwoman claimed to hear
the sounds of fucking all over the world?

161

* • To Ginger Man for dinner and talk Paul and Inara out of going to Bronx for Living Theater. Instead, make a collection of "tiny sounds" - sounds near inaudible (invisible?). For ex. tea-bag lowered into hot water.

• The fantasy version of the Secretary is not <u>another</u> Secretary, but the same, in an altered situation: nude, vulnerable.

• <u>Saturday December 28</u>. 218 lbs.

• Cloudy, foggy. Write first draft of scenario and name piece Typewriter.

• I am the typewriter, I am the object (I am typing on myself). I am the agent, the type writer. I am the news man, I am the printer, I am the control tower.

• Esquire is big pages and tiny type.

• Scraps of the jungle: Xmas tree, rubber plant, hair caught in the plastic holly over the airconditioner, chocolate candy.

• <u>Sunday December 29</u>. 218 lbs.

• Windy, partly cloudy.

• Rejected "office" construction in studio as photo subject, dismantled it and resolved to find actual site. Should we not walk around, our troupe with our objects, find offices, walk in, perform quickly (be photographed), and quickly disappear.

• Double exposure of an office site: day and night. Facts of the day (waking habits) superimposed on facts of the night (sleeping habits, or office after dark). Office workers hooded like the machines, desk-tops both cluttered and bare. Fantasy superimposed on reality, but the superimposition itself treated concretely, like nature.

162

- Like vision, the photo is both real and unreal, but it _is_ real.

- Monday December 30. 219 lbs.

- Clear cold and sunny. Energetic canvassing of offices. "May I see your office?" Manufacturer's Hanover, 57th and 5th; 1st National, Park Ave., 12 floor; Philip Johnson; Irving Trust, 480 Lexington; Family Circle Magazine; J. Walter Thompson, all floors; Unterberg, Towbin, 61 Broadway; etc. Noted program and character of music in lobby of Pepsi-Cola Bldg.

- All offices unsuitable, return discouraged, but later, on way to Post Office, catch sight of office across 14th St. Peek in and find it perfect - it defines the office Ive been looking for.

- In afternoon and evening make giant pencil and a typewriter eraser.

- Tuesday December 31. 217 lbs.

- Cloudy, threat of snow.

- Visit the office selected with photographers Jim and Earl, wait and interview with officers for permission. Accumulating evidence of puritan functionalism. Assembly-line impressionist paintings. Told this is the busiest day of the year in the office. Permission squeezed out.

- Return at 2:30 with small troupe quickly obtained, three in costume. Proceed with increasing disruption of office routine, comments and curiosity. Had hoped office workers would ignore us.

- Proceed to "lie down on the job", on a desk I clear. Had hoped office workers would ignore us, but sense of disruption increases,

comments, loud speculations etc. Lying on my back, I see only the soundproofing of the ceiling. As a specimen member of the audience, am covered, tied, and given the giant pencil and eraser to hold.

· Sweat very much leaving a pattern of moisture on the desk top, but inside am tranquil

· Tranquility continues on return to studio through the rest of day and on into new calendar year.

164

- <u>THEORY AND PREPARATION</u>:

- Early thoughts: the pattern of rectangles.

- Page or two of notes, typed, spoken + drawn and clipped.

- Drawing of boss's costume - others', secretaries'

- Drawing of the boss's soft office.

- Drawing of a giant pencil and typewr. eraser.

- I work up the boss's activities in my office (at studio + on sites). Photo and account.

- I visit a stationery store. Photo and account.

- I study a watercooler, filming it. Photo and account.

- I study a desktop full of office equipment. Photo and account.

- I select players. Account.

- Studying office behavior. Coffee lady. Account.

- LIMITS OF THE MEDIUM (PAGES) AND TIME: CONSTRUCTION AND OBTAINING OF PROPS ELIMINATED. SUGGESTIONS AND ACCOUNTS ONLY. NO PHOTOS EXC. CLIPS.

- <u>SCENARIO</u>:

- TYPOGRAPHICAL

- Sounds and words (to be said and recorded) in column beside the scenario proper.

- WHAT TO SAY (ACCOUNT) Transcripts.

- SOUNDS <u>DESCRIBED</u>

- NATURE OF PAGE AS MEDIUM - SOUND MUST BE IMAGINED

- <u>THE USE OF PHOTOS</u>:

- Act in photo studio

- Comparison of drawn or clipped proposal with actual execution.

165

Set of photos. Before/After - Fantasy/reality. Event/subli-
mation of event. Photo one, photo two.

- Also: Actual event - fantasy - sublimation. 1. photo - 2. clips,
etc. - 3. photo

- PHOTO = REAL

- Also: what I see (photo 1) - what other sees (photo 2)

- what I imagine - what other imagines

- The period of preparation <u>with</u> others in which I receive the
material of others, events are created by others. My prepared
material is cross-bred with that of others.

- Appeal of the photo is that its both real and fantasy Like vision
the photo is both real and unreal, but it is real.

- Which scenario to print: the unreal or real, or both?

- Entrance of audience + TYING UP

- A dirty secretary

- Secretary costumes

- (I direct.)

- Leg behavior. BODY OFFICE BEHAVIOR.

- Contents of a drawer shown

- How to wash floor and desk, pursuing spectators into chairs.

- Installation of tape recorders on thighs. or radios

- Birth of a phone.

- Typewriter behavior

- How to bend over (FILE)

- Tying up of audience

- Use of desk lamp

- Disposal of boss. ATTACK ON ME. SMASHING OF OFFICE.

- <u>GRAND VIEW OF FINALE</u>:

- Act on site. Draw PHOTO ON SITE.

- Deafening sounds described

- Boss smashing office

- All asleep etc. on desks.

- Big Screens with images. STRIP IN.

- Add: Interpretation

- add: Expense list.

- Set: Site

- Props Costumes: draw

- can fake hidden audience in big view.

- Sound machinery will not be necessary for paper presentation.

- Editor and Layout - who? what specialist?

- a. SELECT

  b. INTERPRET

- cast: why not just 12 members of staff of <u>Family Circle</u> fex.? as Tom suggested

- add: <u>Audience</u>:

- schools are on vacation - need only about 50

- Eat

- part of it all is a point of view of E. "literary" "chic", to be seen, superficial.

- translucent plastic - soft office - pushed about.

- paper desks, to be crushed

- large office obj? pencil fex.

- sexuality of the stationery store

- place w. balcony - like Palm gardens. Cheetah now

- a place demanding absolute darkness, absolute silence

- Aspen 1967-68 - series of acts in rel. to society. didactic

- cubicles? thus private

- what is dominant experience now?

- analysis

- (Draft board)

- in ea. an aud. member who is "visited"

- "office"

- "bathroom"

- LIGHT + SOUND

- Light sees sound hears

- Searchlites shine thru?

- (Carolyn Brown)

- Canvas ADRIADNE

168

- Cubicles

- LABYRINTH

- walk over

- burst thru

- carpenters

- ways to handle large audience. several perfs

- audience sort of sneaks up on information

- at the offices of Electronic Design. (humanoid)

- could use this BOY SCOUTS camp? Sanita Hills, Rte. 22, near

  Pawling.

- why not use the people _in_ the office?

- rulers

- anti-act: sleep, snore.

- sitting with B.C. - my model human

- out to a bar or for coffee - abrupt change

- Who will be the audience now?

- Rehabilitation of adj. "sterile", used by Hedley. "surgical"?

- War and sleep (see quotes in Sleep book)

- Typically perverse: faced with a piece to be photographed, I

  prescribe darkness (outer space) and sound (music of the spheres)

- In office: crippled messengers, coffee-ladies, elevators

- Scavenger hunts of the 30s

- Set up an office and the office becomes the record of the

  preparation of the piece

- Lecturelike piece: archaeology of the happening

- In my office now I dont know which fantasy to indulge, that of

169

Private eye or analyst. I wait - no customers.

- The day I arrive there is a fire next door (room 1404) and a man

  dies of smoke inh. The odor of the fire lingers

- Squander money

- Night before, dreamt of a flaming cemetery

- Armory - bunks?

- Cruel fantasies

- Site

- A large area with desks and office machinery and fluorescent

  lights. Also a place that can be made completely dark.

- Secretaries or teachers (nurses)

- Emphasizing sound and sleep (no sound)

- Issue information on mimeograph sheets

- Office party The office after hours

- Hospital/school/cemetery/office - repeated rectangles morgue

- RM calls my cards on the wall an "information retrieving system"

- Information jargon

- Sonnabend said Americans go to movies mainly for information

- Granada typewriter

- Incidents for an Office

- Heavy breathing

- sirens

- thunder (outdoors indoors - the papers will get wet)

- glass breaks

- fire

- a burglary

- snoring

- parade

- bad jokes very loud

- gas leak

- Hayden Pub. Co. typewriter

- First day at the office. A frightening sensation.

* - Marge – playing grownup

* - Win – elimination of vowels Egyptian f. ex. CPLY

- Studios in different parts of the city office, church, factory....

- The time was chosen carefully: Xmas – from Store to Office

* - Recollections: Velsicol (office party) and 44 Bellevue Place

- Office fantasies

- Instead of diaries or notes, just record on tape each day and

- have it transcribed by secy.

- The theme is connection (esp. here in the electronics industry) connection between art and nonart soc. worlds (and everything else) the awful flowing together

- My own data processing, _myself an office_

- Photogs idea of what he wd here photo.

- Barbaras

CONVISER

KLEINBERG

- toothache

- mating systems

- data processing

- PRESENTS

171

- OHMS

- the repetition of rectangles elect.

- fur

- 54 st.: St. Peters, 1st Nat'l, Elysee (Monkey room) MOMA, Rhodes, Moon dog, this corner

- a new language

- Humanoids

- meaning in hpgs are they anti-meaning only as means to new meaning?

- the cause is poetic rather than political

- some reading thinking

- the projection (unsuccessful) of the "formal" "abstract" "nonfunctional" or diverted (to other functions) world of my experience

- now a look at the competition. I feel way behind.

- politics

- nudity

- In Chi I was a member of the audience at a theater piece

- non-directed activity amidst directed.

- office is something one takes a stand about...BC's remarks

- like the painting in office.

- recount activity end of day.

- pour coffee

- dial 9

- watch clock - 1:30.

- jokes, 'Polish' - why?

- heels

- laughter

- male/female

- typewriter cleaning.

- hardon in an office.

- paper from top.

- piano

- raised voices

- singing

- dialing

- sound can be described not photoed anyway.

- Midtown needs gentle sounds.

- Leningrad victims.

- Cover people w. sheets

- set up a one big shot, big symbol.

- the apparitions

- bomb shelter victims shores of darkness = office

- watching symbols apparitions

- (Christ) FAN

- combine religious + mundane "opposites". double objects

- the white fleet of muse/secretaries (all black)

- color fex. use of what is as material w. no more feel for it than
  if it were material - or with feel for it as material + feel for
  what one _does_ w. it

- Induction center

- Immigration office (Christo)

173

- Steno pool

- wax cylinder

* - Janis Ian - WAIF

- Nite of the Living Dead

- GHOUL

- Ulysses

- Joe sleeps

- laugh rec.

- loneliness

- the water-man LA.

- sneezing

- GOD

- office

- Orson Welles, Kane, Rosebud

- Computer

- I am a computer.

- buried look of office after dark.

- wash floor

- draw sound

- sound is so important

* - Joe called, interrupting an office party.

- Joe describes his project.

- Tom arrives: "I ran". "What did you run from"? "I ran from that
  fucking office".

- Night Tripper

* - Lita not victim

*   ·   phone in tomb

·   M.B.E. phone nr.

·   Nurses ("I a woman")

*   ·   "Mistaken Identity"

·   Evenings

·   Light = Information

·   "throw some light on it"

·   ULYSSES

·   Swineherd disg.

·   at night she undoes it

·   <u>nurse</u> is washing feet. scar.

·   Oedipus

·   Penelope knows

·   Return to the body. Reunion

·   C.S. (Christian Science) data processing of God. etc.

·   Recapitulation + Reading Room.

·   relation of object to word.

·   word = shit

·   office situation

·   random situation

·   forced interaction

·   BOSS

·   Julie talks about office

·   Office + Eurydice

·   Morpheus +

·   Orifice

175

- LABYRINTH

- VICTORIA = ARIADNE

- Theater of religious perception thru observation of the mundane

- office manual.

- garb goes out mail (sperm) comes in.

- dictation

- Penelope envelope

- Soft scissors

- Self as receiving set.

- Dynamite

- phone = x sphincter CUTOFF

- record telephone confusion now

- telephone cord - umbilical

- sitting down or not has become so important.

- HOTLINE

- Pamela Cain - phone operator N.Y. Studio School

- phone = ma or wife or child or a woman delivers a phone from under her skirt.

- Earthquake.

- mother + phone (phone as reporter)

- my pieces usually end in destruction + silence

- it is the same piece + subj. usually is death

- when left alone I make a mess try to attract attent.

- assassination

- airconditioning

- bulbs break lights quiver

176

- <u>Basic units</u>:

  The boss

  cleaning men (bears)

  Sec'y (nurses)

  desks

- intercom

- buzzer

- spill ink on self. red blue

- sec'ys go to boss

- sec's hobbled in some way.

- aud. enters

- a loudspeaker: this is a police sit.! everyone sit down in a chair

- the aud. is tied in the chair

- ea. desk a stage

- fan, tel., typewr., clock, BOSS

- at end covered w. sheets

- on stages: secretaries. TO DO AND READ follow instructions from BOSS. SCHOOL EXERCISE

- in aisles: cleaning men keep floor wet

- CO words

- all masturbating

- Verbal for first time?

- emphasis AURAL

- w. a theme - or based on a text

- a restaurant - things come out of a hole

- this is
  this is not } a hapg.

- cut out letters

- Spelling contest

- mops (maps?)

- massage - contact

- personnel.

- secretarys (or Muses)

- People come in MUZAK is playing

- ea. gets a desk. desk is locked. a little light on ea.

- ea. gets objects. silkscreen sheet of reprods?

- ea. gets instructions on phone

- 1. telephone sound

  2. typewriter sound

  3. Fan - film. gradually lightening image. or silhouette.

- bed time.

- MUZAK again

- TIME big clock.

- Secrecy

- 1st state - expansion

  2nd state - retreat

- History of hpg in objects, events

- Hapg is a diversion of function, or a slowing down of things for analysis.

- The playhouse of the natural (non-human) world.

- Coney Island - audience - coming on stage -

178

- Obtain a stationery store catalogue. Or as w. "Stars" in Wash.,
  which was about souvenirs, take five hundred bucks and squander it
  in a big Stationery store (Strongins fex. or Goldsteins)
- Contents of a drawer (several)
- Opening drawers from upside down. Sitting under a desk. (Old
  typewriters used to emerge from the desk top.
- The big bubble in a watercooler. Film. where?
- paper clips.
- Scatological use of the office in my notes: shitting into a typewriter f. ex.
- Speaking speedwriting
- writing dictation
- in Kaprow the audience participates in tortured still removed
  versions of orgy (sadomaso perversions)
- as in Carolees pieces - exhibitionism or Lebels
- Reference: one of the girly mags stolen by the college students
  had a sequence of a girl tied to an office desk after hours,
  stripped, sucked and fucked.
- the burglary
- At this point - the office fantasy is crossbreeding with bondage
  and masochist fantasy (office masturbation)
- office party w. staged lesbian romps (rumps)
- girl bending for files w. spankings etc.
- Form out of sex, by substitution
- build model
- Big hand (King Kong) reaches down - one impossible act like that,
  one we never could do.

179

- The enlargement of an object thru sound.

- a literary attempt - determined by the medium

- Perfume.

- pencil in mouth.

- makeup haircomb

- body sounds

- machine sounds

- naked bodies vs. furniture

- paths of secretaries in the dark

- paths of sound

- Clips (are) cruel per se.

- Private eye of myself Recall phone scenario fantasy

- Shitting on the floor is a cruel act

- This will be the form of the "bosss" office (artist) my version of
  an office.

- When I get the "board" up (as at Ray Gun) an editor may copy from
  it.

- The studio is useful because the originals for effects are here
  within reach

- Heels in cardboard

- Dust from above covers office

- Studio of old sets The back lot

- Maybe it will come to something very simple:

  A big banquet shot:

  50 people disposed through an office by me impromptu say 50

people from an office even if its not a great overhead view say

in cubicles I arrange ea one a difft way photog walks thru

· Bums? Family Circle? Nudes?

· the recorders can be obtained small enough to strap on thighs but

for Esq they can be just mockups. for a real perf there are small

ones or EAT could build. Earphones or as airline hostesses de-

monstrate

· Incidents developed in oldfashioned loft env. (studio) – whose

better than mine (?) might be good contrast and explain the span

between then and now artist and office and many things (Dec 26)

· Win is gentle placid, could get wig

· Talent contest

· Parody of Courbet

· All art (and office) is about indifference to the woman

· Drawings take time

· Career advice – how to get ahead or short readings by day

by Secretaries of daily career advice

· Charts

· Numbers – the Adding Machine

· Eating lunch brought to the office

· Mechanical activity – fast filing

· Wastebaskets

· Get catalogue of office machinery

· Crushing by a machine (Modern Times dream)

· Girl with typewriter, w. other machines, with pencil sharpener

· Parts of body with machines

(machine as body)

181

- Wind of fan, airconditioning

- Bendings over, as soften seen, kneelings. Views

- 60s are the years when USA sadomasochisticfetishistic soul was turned loose to disrupt sometimes for form but mostly for the sake of disruption We helped turn it loose and we tried harnessing it using it making it productive

- Studio as office.

- The studio version of the office provides improvised metaphors of the actual office, comical improvisations I'll simply purchase ass't shambly office equipment

- Secretary on stage is like the model on stand

- My studio I realize is an office fantasy anyway - even the store - the Ray Gun Mfg Co. had its fantasy

- Andys factory was a later development

- A studio office full of models (secretaries) a la Rodin

- enlarge selected pinups

- An Expense List

- Office jealousy rivalry disruption of routine

- What may be done is to have the whole of the material as presented submitted to analysis - that depends on the magazines attitude towards its readers and policy do they merely show or do they explain?

- The secretaries circulate from the main office to the desk stages, wearing taperecorders playing the sounds of the office (under their skirts?).

182

· The conceptual period now turning requests for tangible things
into instructions, concepts, written provocations. One way to
dispose of the mass of requests

· problem solving.

· The key to the effects of the hapg as I do it lie in my behavior.
They represent my "problems".

· People are appropriate for the "realization" or stimulation of my
fantasy.

· Gloria had it quite right. So what, if form is the outcome...

· My cruel and homosexual fantasies, my punishment and its "forms"

· It shouldnt be a realization of fantasy, it should be a suggestion
or a suppression of fantasy - the mannikin and it shd be american
very sweet in the puritan applepie sense

· Nakedness is just part of the disappearance of the object and
artist

· Women detest fashion mags. Try fash mags for women?

· The fantasies are on the wall in the mind in the magazines
and not for real

· All my perfs are rather violent and involve imposition of
tension between audience and players and space - between all
things and usually involve an explosion of some sort - a relief
followed by silence they are personal, festishistic...

· I was asked to do an analysis of the hapng but I am performing and
noone is watching no ed. that is.

· Audience to be obtained from an office (Tom)

· Manpower Inc.

183

- Copyright piece

- Due to the lack of time the development is telescoped and hurried.

- By the 26th the piece should be moving into sublimated form areas, translating itself into form

- The birth theme

- Christ is mixed up here somewhere

- manger - desk

- Mary - Secretary   secret mary

- Joe

- Incident: destruction of a manger (desk) mentioned before:

- Kienholz's axing of the Trans World desk

- Recall film made as a kid attacking my desk papers in air

- Masochistic fantasy of rending clothes, destruction

- Orpheus-orifice Office as body since all subject matter is essentially body in-body reunion

- PAYROLL

- An office is the "other" place so WC Fields goes to his office away from home (a bar) Dirty Old Man

- The office of the E. Village Other

- Masochistic machine Modern Times

- Information & Masochism

- "Man was the first data processor"

- BOX - the OFFICE

- I think the idea of many rectangles in rows did come from the card catalogue. of my works I am preparing

- Office - the Brain (Hat) The hat house hat rack

184

- Office is the mind as I told Barb rel of mind to body abstraction to things

- the office in back of the store is growing (the brain is growing to dominate the work over the visceral)

- Some Cruel events:

  Blood in the (draftboard) files

  Secretary wrestles with colossal typewriter eraser

  A ruler creeps up the Secys thighs

  The Secy delivers a huge bloody telephone on a desktop. The cord is cut with an office scissors

- Add:

  Try naked secretaries finding the mouth of the audience with candies.

- After all what is more subversive to an office than total darkness? Or to a magazine page?

- Like in cartoon strips black panels with sound noises.

- The darkness may be my mind evoking the fantasies

- recollection of "sounds heard" of childhood (secrets) suggested by the Dr.

- Also womb thoughts etc. (see notes)

- Being a bad contrary boy (so cruel and self-effacing) is so necessary

- Tricks like these are why literary agents may not be useful to a slippery artist.

- Happenings really are dead (mine anyway) and I cant perform a resuscitation and cant work up enough enthusiasm for a reconstruction in any depth.

185

- Was it an Anouilh play where a mad woman could hear the sounds of fucking all over the world?

- If not total darkness, partiality of illumination, which characterized happenings. Yes - the light effect <u>as it will appear on the page</u> is vital - that it should feel like the H itself.

- it corresponds to: other minds in a dark room evoking the fantasies (all this has come from the sensitivity to sound engendered by Chamberlains "dead" radio, Larry's walking etc.)

- The pix of me shows me from the outside - the building and the inside darkness invisible (is it dark in there?) thinking invisible and imaginably dreadful thoughts. Visible are the departurepoints of my fantasy, and some sublimated realizations of it.

- Chiaroscuro

- Imagination

- The office then the womb or brain - inside body in what ever way See my yearbook illustration of inside/outside

- Feeding all the materials including most practical ones like the weather and the conditions of the editorial etc. etc. the lack of time etc. this is a proper? solution.

- The project must also be formulated as a page plan a composition, layout. The Statement should be self-deluded, ie. the rationalization. The truth should be evident but unstated. This is not an interpretation but a presentation.

- Subject and verb like the early lists in 1959 of "things" which led to the happening

186

- In add to scenario an interview can be done or better an editing of the notes I am putting up

- The Seance was the model for the happening in the store and of Blackouts (Illuminations) objects

- Light and sound are the components of a happening

- not a "sterile" office - that word is not precise.

- We have in this site a "minimal" office, which means a practical and yet <u>strangely metaphysical</u> place, stripped to function and austerely puritanical, with the barest gesture towards organic material: an Xmas tree, a rubber plant, an impressionist landscape. Minimal content and minimal form.

- The title not until at the end where the scenario appears

- title article <u>Archaeology of the Happening</u> which will pick up nicely on the body facing page

- Grey matter, set the theory thoughts in greys and blacks.

- diary in red?

- duatone alterations of clip photos

- On p 3 the word DATA should appear

- Add use of candy?

- "A long time ago (as NY time goes) Oldenburg did his happenings... Here he tries to recall the method..."

- Starts then w. my statement, theoretical and clear and changes gradually into fragments by the third page it is looser and in type or handwriting

- I am the typewriter the object and the agent keys on the

typewriter - desk arrangement the hapg is about time. wound in the office use of certain random texts

- all office furniture catalogues have abstr. ptgs on walls.
- Crossbreeding of sex and office
- body and machine
- A man and a woman in an office Man Being recorded by the woman
- relation thru machine
- Take this situation and work on it Improvise with single "sec'y" or "filing clerk"
- Two secretaries, dressed alike, with rubber band and blanket. We go from one office to another with Jim and repeat the event of lying down on top of a desk being covered with a blanket and fastened with a rubber band (lying down on the job).
- (Interesting that the operating room image introduced weeks ago is still there)
- Blanket like a typewriter cover (vinyl?) Typewriter eq. body
- Pencil and eraser in hand
- Add: If words are used either recorded or spoken (as the candy is passed round) use the phrases and exercises of the touch type writing manual: some examples.
- The hapg always becomes for me a facing of self The fear of transposing fantasy into reality or the substitutions necessary for me to achieve secret satisfaction (?)
- For this reason, a kind of lecture on my theory of art
- BR passed on to me RMs comment that I could handle a lot of in- formation - well, cant any body-machine that wants to?

188

- Hands everywhere

- A lot of wiring wiring that goes in the floor wiring everywhere

- tragedy of an interrupted circuit

- Labyrinth Ariadne - wiring

- Parody of electronic diagram for performance action

- Sets of leg behavior, crossing etc.

- Clipboard

- stenopads

- makeup

- Licking stamps

- Clean shirts on men and black ties

- Mud in the office

- Big pencil (again)

- everything has a sound

- Night is superimposed on day The audience sleeps on the desk-tops
  covered like the silent machines

- Audience superimposed on subject

- Fantasy superimposed on reality

- I associate small type w. Esq.

- Liquor holds out the promise of inspiration, daring to act,
  excitement... relief from selfcriticism, escape from boredom...
  or so it speaks.. The q. is whether I can function as an artist
  without stimulants. this was a temptation one is tempted every
  time inspiration leaves to drink

- the nude version very simply is the fantasy version secy

- Costume solutions by copout - nudity dressed in skin its a
  cost. too

189

- Enlargements

- Girlie mags crossbred with machinery and office mags stationery
  cat's

- A gentle image

- Kinds of office

- Like the Velsicol memory

- green walls

- black marbled linoleum

- grey desks + files

- The two memory offices: The Swed. Cons. at Bellevue Place and
  the Velsicol office (E Ross Humphrey, Bill Kauer etc) and their
  office party.

- Barb C. measure.

- Assembling "Secretaries"

- A matter of telling the woman in time Mon so they could get the
  standard male office attire by Tuesday, New Years Eve

- And telling them to stand by for notification of where by Tue AM.
  To set aside the PM

- Expenses: salaries plus costumes, food whatever

- Use of office no doubt free.

190

- <u>Tiny sounds</u>
- paper clip is slid onto paper
- spindle point penetrates paper
- hat hung up
- pencil writing
- secretary kneeling
- biting into sandwich (lettuce, bacon)
- combing of hair
- application of lipstick
- earring against the skin
- tongue stroking teeth
- pencil tapped on teeth
- newspaper pages turned
- teabag lowered into hot water
- adjusting of glasses on nose
- suppressed fart in a desk chair
- an erection rising
- taking off a shoe
- licking a stamp
- ripping open an envelope
- searching a valise
- chewing candy
- paper crumpled (too loud a sound?)
- scissors cut paper
- rubber band is spread
- pushing a button

- (Tiny sounds cont'd)

- adjusting stockings, pants

- filing

- grinding out a cigarette

- spilling of ink

- changing a ribbon

- one leg crossed over another

- sharpening pencil (sound heard round the world)

- bubbles in a watercooler (too loud?)

- (cracking a safe?)

192

- THE OFFICE

- (Sleep

  Data

  Information)

- VERY FIRST DRAFT

- <u>THE OFFICE</u>

- A large square room filled with desks, tops empty, in neat rows
  (about 50 - limit of the audience). Audience enters. A loudspeaker guides them to the fifty chairs placed before the desks.
  The source of the voice may be concealed. Police attitude (dis-
  cussed w. Lita & see Cage) - The Boss. Tells audience to sit
  down in chairs. After the audience sits down, they are bound by
  rubber bands in the chairs by 25 office workers and 25 Secretaries
  (in Massage these were Nurses). There are also 5 Cleaning People
  who, when the audience enters, are washing the floors with a lot
  of water and wiping the desks. They slop the water at the feet of
  the audience which hurries them to their desk-chairs, where the
  members of the audience may sit with their feet drawn up. The
  secretaries wear galosches (or are barefoot?).

- Each desk is a stage.

- There are four screens, one on each side of the room. One shows
  a Fan, one a typewriter, one a telephone, one a clock, in huge
  format and in motion - perhaps selected details of each instrument
  are also shown.

- The Boss-Executive (Executives?) - has a desk in front of the

other desks or in the center. He is concealed. The City Desk, or information center, control tower..He may appear only as silhouette or in a costume or may rise out. While the cleaning men keep the floors wet, the secretaries obtain their orders from the boss and execute the orders on the desks before the bound spectators. Perhaps the secretaries should be hobbled in some way like crippled messengers. Blindfolded? The secretaries are given instructions, things to do or to read, to laugh secretarial laughter, to talk to audience. Information. Sounds of the phone and sounds of the typewriter, magnified, are heard from time to time. The clock rings and occasionally a blast of dynamite. Voyeur situation, control situation. Each desk may have an inter-com or a buzzer.

· Messengers arrive and there is a lady selling coffee.

· Items in the drawers.

· Incidents at the office. Instructions to Secretaries and Pre-recorded material attached to their bodies (thighs), upper thighs.

· Heel sounds.

· This whole vision which is vast must be brought down to the level of the possible. Ludicrously to the level of my fantasy - it is just me in the office. (Where did all the people go?).

· A photo representing the essentially personal nature of my happenings.

· In that respect they are like my sculpture.

· I fired myself.

· It's _me_, the "boss" <u>in an office</u> (long ago and/or now) receiving

messages, sending messages, writing fantasies, and dirtying up the place. The boss' rage - he storms out. Bicycles. The personal emphasis of my happenings is unavoidable. Authoritarianism of art. Im working with that much more than in the last few. The early ones were very personal. Smashes his office

195

- <u>PARTS</u>:

  COMING TO WORK

  WORK

  COFFEE BREAK

  WORK

  LUNCH HOUR

  WORK

  QUITTING TIME

  OFFICE PARTY

  PAY DAY

  HIRING - FIRING

  BURGLARY

  WASHROOM

  AFTER HOURS.

  SEC IN OFFICE.

- As years have gone by Ive become too analytical about my hapng activity.

- The audience now is imagined to be too demanding.

- Use of a calendar.

- Use of desk lamps. Sec's examine selvs.

- For esq. purposes the sound will be represented by drawings. The typical desk chair relation can be set up, several other all characters + events set up in photographs. Perhaps four desk setups can be repeated in a collage photograph, and all the ingredients thus brought together without the use of an actual office.

196

- Closeups and a long shot.

- The piece ends with covering up the audience like the covering
of typewriters at the end of the day. Underwood. The secretaries
sleep on the desks, and the sound of the <u>Fan</u> dominates all. The
waking up and release is accompanied by Muzak-like sound.

- In the actual aural perf. tape recorders can be involved. The
secretaries can record items and leave them to be heard by the
captive audience while they return for more information. Jokes +
jargon. Snoring. Laughing. A mimeograph machine may be used to
grind out instructions. The secretaries will use office supplies:
pencils, ribbons, pencil sharpeners, stamps, and ink (which they
may spill on themselves). Dirtying up the office. Paste and
Scissors.

- Use of light: total darkness at one point, in the sleep scene
and weak light at first entrance?

- Feet in wastebaskets

- Possible add. business:

- Use of desk props in any way - to handle - Fex? like a typewriter
eraser...

- Adriadne bit - the Sec's unwind office string to find their way
back if necessary

197

- <u>Draft 1</u>

- The Office, or The Typewriter, an anti-visual piece

- A large room in a modern office, unsectioned: one large room, full of desks in center, in rows, about thirty six grey metal desks with sharp corners and smooth surfaces. Office equipment. High ceiling. A totally indoor office, no windows, capable of being totally darkened, the utter darkness in which sounds become extremely tangible; the eye sense shifts to the ear, middle of the forest at the darkest part of night.

- When the audience enters the Office, it is brightly lit with fluorescent light and piped-in, calming midtown music is playing. "Poor Butterfly". Aides, called "Secretaries" - about six men and six women, in proper office attire, show the members of the audience (formerly "spectators") the position they will take during the performance, ·which is: a member of the audience will lie down on a desk-top (the desk-tops have been cleared) will be covered with a blanket and will be tied to the desk by a large rubber band. Lift one end? The secretaries first demonstrate and then bed down and tie the member of the audience. The number of the audience is limited to the number of desk-tops.

- Courteous attire identical, masculine: white shirt, black tie. About same size. My size?

- Floor being cleaned.

- When all members of the audience have been fastened to desk-tops, all illumination is completely extinguished. The Secretaries have returned to stations alongside twelve coatracks placed at

the edges of the room. For a few minutes in total darkness, the
soothing music goes on, while the Secretaries remove their
clothing and hang it on the racks.

· S turn on desk machines.

· Each nude Secretary then straps on a tape recorder (twelve taperecorders with pre-recorded material have been hung on the coatracks), and, at the moment the calming music ends, the Secretaries
turn on the machines. Each Secretary begins traveling slowly
through the darkness to the coat-rack opposite, through the desks
in the center of the room.

· Around the room are amplifiers delivering additional sound. The
sound carried by the Secretaries and from the amplifiers consists
of concrete sounds of the Office (no words), half derived from
machinery (f. ex. the typewriter), half from the body-object
sounds and an occasional word (f. ex. throat-clearing). While the
level of sound carried by the Secretaries remains the same, the
sound from the amplifiers is machinery, which gradually becomes
louder, and is more and more dominated by the sound of typing.
This period of sound in darkness should last at least twenty
minutes - which will seem a very long time. The sound should become "deafening" - pass beyond the level of loudness where the ear
seems to shut off, and a sort of sleep sets in, where for the
protection of the body, sound becomes silence. Then, abruptly,
the sound ends both from the amplifiers and from the recorders on
the Secretaries. There is five minutes of "silence", in which
actual sounds become manifest: the breathing and shifting about

of the audience, the dressing again of the Secretaries, small
accidents; and now the ear acquires supersensitivity, hears f. ex.
the small sound of jewelry. At the end of this period, the
fluorescent lights quiver on, and the Office is again full of
harsh light. As when the plane again contacts the earth, the
calm music resumes. The Secretaries, clothed again, courteously
undo, unbed the members of the audience.

The performance is over.

200

· <u>Draft one</u>

· The Office an anti-visual happening

· The description of the piece can be run in text. I guess thats

needed:

· My talk!

· This is an entirely aural piece.

· An office with a number of desks (at least fifty) and one which

can be completely darkned is chosen. The audience ea. chooses a

desk and is bedded down there/strapped to a desk with blankets by

"secretaries". The lights are completely doused and the sound

emanates from the circulating naked secretaries and from loud-

speakers placed under the desks in the desks and around the room.

the secs pick their way slowly and carefully in the dark. larger

sounds like the typewriter gradually dominate and become extreme-

ly loud when the very loud sound has continued a length of time

it stops abruptly/the lights go on and soft music and the audience

is unbedded + released with the aid of the secs

· to soft music

· the secs + clerks remove their clothing + don tape recorders

The office door is shut. The stench of heated disinfectant

fills the room, spread by the wall fans

· The wall fans spread the stench of heated disinfectant which fills

the room.

· When all members of the audience are tied in place, the Floor-

washers depart with their equipment, not bothering to wipe up any

pools of water they have made.

201

- The Secretaries return to their posts by the hat trees.

- The fluorescent lamps flicker off, one row after another leaving the office invisible.

- The soft music played during the positioning of the audience, continues for a short while, then stops abruptly.

- At this moment, the sounds of the office machinery, the body in the office and the office object effects taped on the recorders hidden in the desks should begin, and also the sound of typing carried by the amplifier. At this moment, too, the Secretaries switch on the tape recorders hanging on the hat trees. The Secretaries remove the office costume, hang it on the trees and strap the operative recorders around their waists. They then begin a blind journey through the maze of desks and office equipment, using their hands and feet and other parts of the body to find their way to a hat tree on the opposite side of the office. This trip will take fifteen minutes.

- At the end of the five minute period of large scale typing sound, each Secretary should have found another tree and another costume. The Secretaries unstrap the recorders, hang them up and dress again during the five minute period of silence that follows.

- The absolute darkness continues, but without recorded sound. Members of the audience, adjusting their ears to the new condition, begin to hear the tiny real sounds in the space. Breathing, coughing and the sounds of others turning and twisting in their uncomfortable condition. They hear the change in the pockets of the Secretaries' pants as they dress. and, their

senses overstimulated by the exposure to the opposite extreme, may

begin to imagine normally unhearable, miniature sounds

· and, aurally overworked, may begin to imagine normally unhearable

miniature sounds, such as the dipping of a tea bag into hot water

or the sliding on to paper of a metal clip.

· The five minute period of silence ends suddenly with the relight-

ing of the fluorescent lamps. They quiver on and the soft music

resumes where it ended - reminding one of the moment when the

wheels of the plane recontact the runway and pick up again the

soothing sound, as natural a fixture as the clouds

· They quiver on and the audience rubs its eyes. In a moment

reminiscent of that moment when the plane makes contact again with

the runway and with the soothing music which blankets the

continent like a natural element

· The Secretaries release the audience. The piece is over.

· The following assistants will be needed to perform the piece:

1) twelve "Secretaries", six male, six female.

2) two pairs of "Floorwashers", male.

3) several uncostumed assistants to handle lighting and sound.

· All the "Secretaries" regardless of size and sex wear the same

costume - a pair of black men's pants with black suspenders, a

white shirt, and a black and white polka-dot tie. They wear

nothing underneath. The garments are all of the same size. The

pants are 30 inches long in the leg and 36 inches around at the

waist. The shirts are 35 inches long in the sleeve and 16 inches

around the neck.

· These are the author's sizes.

· The pockets of the pants are to be filled with small change.

· The "Floorwashers" wear grey coveralls. They carry big mops and
huge buckets of hot smoking water containing a large dose of
strong-smelling disinfectant.

· All assistants wear gym shoes.

· Each apparatus is provided with a previously recorded tape, ready
to play, of a mixture of the following sounds:

1) sounds of office machinery - typing, adding, dialing etc.

2) sounds of the body in the office - sneezing, scratching,
yawning, etc.

3) sounds of the object activity in the office - stamping,
crumpling, clicking etc.

· Tape recorders with the same material are also fastened under each
desk-top or placed in a drawer of each desk. There are turned on
just before the audience enters the office.

· Ten minutes are required to tie the members of the audience to the
desk-tops. Therefore the first ten minutes of these tapes are
blank. An amplifier capable of very loud sound is placed in the
office at whatever spot is determined to be the most effective.
When the audience enters the office, taped musical arrangements
such as those heard in lobbies and elevators of office buildings
are playing through the amplifier. After ten minutes, the tape
changes to a recording of the typewriting <u>of this scenario</u>

· The sound of this scenario being typed continues for twenty

minutes, and should end together with the sounds of the portable tape recorders and those concealed in the desks. But, unlike the other recorded sounds, the sound of the typing increases gradually in volume. After fifteen minutes, the sound of the typing is extremely loud and this volume is maintained for five minutes, which will seem a very long time.

- The office space will resound like a battlefield. The contact of a character with paper will sound like a shell bursting. The little pauses for thought while writing the scenario will become huge spaces charged with tense anticipation of the next crash.

- When sound becomes too loud, the body tends to fall asleep.

- Each member of the audience is given two large objects to hold – a giant pencil and a giant typewriter eraser.

- These are reproduced from originals made by the author. A set of objects is placed on each desk-top, before the audience enters the office, along with 1) a brown Army blanket and 2) a length of thick rope or a giant version of a rubber band.

- The action with the mops and water should be directed at the fine shoes of the entering audience members, with the objective of encouraging them to protect themselves by climbing on the desks. Their doing so will be suggested by the twelve Secretaries, who begin first to demonstrate and then to situate the members of the audience on the desk-tops. Each audience member is covered with the Army blanket and tied with the rope or giant rubber band, around the whole desk. Once tied, they are given the giant pencil and typewriter eraser to hold in their hands.

- The audience is told (not by announcement but quite intimately, by each Secretary) that the giant objects are very fragile and not to be released. Releasing them would cause them to fall on the floor to become wet, to be trampled or to be shattered. The audience members can determine with their fingers that the giant objects are indeed very fragile.

- There is no alternative for a decent person, and in the total darkness of the performance, the holding of the objects may reduce anxiety. The details of the objects may be explored by the fingers as a pass-time.

206

- Draft 2

- <u>The Typewriter</u>

- An anti-visual theater piece, Dec. 1968.

- <u>Site</u>:

- A large square room with high ceilings - an accounting office. An office of maximum desolation - austerely functional and penny-pinching. Minimal grey metal desks and the necessary machinery at each desk.

- A hard floor of black and white marbled linoleum. Walls painted a moribund green. A soundproofed ceiling with rows of fluorescent lights.

- The desks are grouped close to one another in the center of the room. The desks are cleared, except of telephones and other office machinery: typewriters, accounting machines etc. which are under covers.

- Around the room, several wall-fans, rotating and turning.

- The office must be without windows, or it must be possible to mask the windows completely. Proper execution of the piece requires absolute darkness.

- The number of the audience will depend on the number of desks: one audience member to a desk.

- <u>Preparations</u>:

- Twelve identical coatracks to be obtained and placed at regular intervals near the walls of the room. On each rack, a small tape-recorder fitted w. a belt so that it can be fastened around the waist.

207

- On each recorder, ready to play, a tape of previously recorded sounds, alternating sounds of the office (machinery and objects effects, f. e x. dialing, paper crumpled) with sounds of the body (f. ex. throat-clearing).

- Each tape a different sequence, but all tapes of the same duration - twenty minutes, all to finish in unison.

- Under each desk-top or in a drawer of each desk, a recorder loaded with the same material.

- The desk recorders are turned on as the audience enters. Therefore the first ten minutes of the tapes (about the time it will take to fasten the audience to the desks) are blank.

- Somewhere in the space - where it will be most effective, an amplifier capable of very loud sound attached to a tape recorder. The tape to be played: ten minutes of soft music ("Poor Butterfly", etc. in mild, saccharine arrangements), followed by a recording of the typing of this scenario twenty minutes long, timed to end with the other taped sounds; followed by a silence of 5 min. and then resumption of soft music.

- Control of the loudness of the sound in three stages: 1) at the level of the other taped sounds, for ten minutes; 2) a middle level, definitely louder than the other taped sounds, for five minutes; 3) a very loud level, for five minutes.

- The sound of the typewriter at the loudest level is like a battle-field. The pauses (for thought in writing the scenario) become anxious anticipations of the next unpredictable burst of sound.

- In sound, five minutes is a long time. In a previous run-thru

members of the audience told me that, when the sound became unendurable, they found themselves falling asleep.

- For each member of the audience, a giant pencil and a giant typewriter eraser to be made by the author and duplicated. These will be placed on the desk-tops along with a brown army blanket and a thick length of rope or simulated giant rubber band, fex. a cut up tire tube.

- <u>Cast and Costume</u>:

- Twelve aides, called "Secretaries", six male and six female and two pairs of "Floorwashers", male, are required.

- The Secretaries are dressed in the same costume: black men's pants with black suspenders, a white shirt and a polka-dot tie. They wear nothing underneath. All the clothing is the same size: pants: 36 in. waist, 30" long; shirt: 16 in. neck, 35 in. arm.

- These are the author's sizes.

- The Floorwashers wear grey overalls, carry mops and huge buckets of smoking hot water mixed with strong-smelling detergent.

- Secretaries and Floorwashers both wear gym shoes.

- Some non-costumed assistants for sound and lighting also required.

- The pantspockets of the Secretaries will be full of change.

- <u>Action</u>

- The audience is kept in a waiting room or corridor outside the office until preparations are complete.

- When the audience enters, timing of the piece begins. The door to the office is shut. The office is brightly lit, the soft music is playing. Office objects etc. are in place on the desks, and

the Secretaries stand by their coathangers, smiling. The Floorwashers are aggressively wetting the linoleum. They encourage the
audience to get on top of the desks. The Secretaries help in
placing the members of the audience, by demonstrating and then by
assisting. Each member of the audience is covered with the
blanket, tied, and then given the giant office objects to hold.

- The audience is told that the giant objects are very delicate -
which they are - and that they are not to let them drop on the
floor. Since there is no room on the desk, there is no other
alternative but to hold on to them. In the darkness they will
provide a certain security, and may be explored with the fingers
as a pass-time.

- The stench of heated disinfectant fills the room. When the
audience is tied in place, the Floorwashers leave. The
Secretaries return to their coat-rack stations. The fluorescent
lights flicker off one by one until the room is totally dark.

- The soft music continues a while, then stops abruptly.

- If the timing is correct, this moment will coincide with the start
of the taped sounds from the desk-recorders and the amplifier.
The Secretaries switch on their recorders and undress, hanging
their costumes on the coatrack. They strap the recorders around
their waists, and begin a journey in the darkness through the
group of desks to the opposite coat-rack.

- This trip will take twenty minutes - the period of escalating
sound. When the loudest sound period ends, the Secretaries should
find themselves across the room at a coat-rack. They remove

the recorder and dress again, during the five minute period of silence that follows.

· The total darkness continues. All recorded sound is off. Instead the audience begins to hear small actual sounds: sounds of the fan, sounds of the Secretaries dressing (sound of the change in their pockets), breathing, sounds made by the audience, twisting in their uncomfortable situations etc. The five-minute silent period ends suddenly, with the relighting of the fluorescent lights - they quiver on and the soft recorded music resumes - as when the airliner again contacts the earth.

· The Secretaries untie the audience. The piece is finished.

211

- THE TYPEWRITER

  an anti-visual piece for an Office

  Dec. 1968

- Copyright C.O.

- Could this be made more visual? Could it be printed over some

  pale material? Color paper?

- <u>Site</u>

- A large square room with high ceiling - an accounting office. An

  office of maximum desolation - austerely functional and penny-

  pinching. Minimal grey metal desks. A hard floor covered with

  black and white marbled linoleum. Walls painted a moribund green.

  A sound-proofed ceiling with rows of fluorescent lights. The

  desks are placed close to one another in the center of the room.

  The desks are cleared, except of telephones. Office chairs and

  smaller tables with office machinery - typewriters, accounting

  machines etc., which are under covers, clutter the aisles.

  Around the room, several wall-fans, rotating and turning. The

  office selected must be without windows, or it must be possible to

  mask the windows completely. Proper execution of the piece re-

  quires absolute darkness. The number of the audience will depend

  on the number of desks: one audience member to a desk.

- <u>Preparations</u>

- Twelve identical hat trees are placed at regular intervals near

  the walls around the room. On each tree is hung a small, portable

  tape recorder, fitted with a belt so that it can be fastened to a

  body around the waist. Each apparatus is provided with a previ-

ously recorded tape, ready to play, of a mixture of the following

sounds:

1) sounds of office machinery - typing, adding, dialing, etc.

2) sounds of the body in the office - sneezing, scratching,

   yawning, etc.

3) sounds of object activity in the office - stamping, crumpling,

   clicking, etc.

· Tape recorders with the same material are also fastened under each

desk-top, or placed in a drawer of each desk. These are turned on

just before the audience enters the office. Ten minutes are

needed to tie the members of the audience to the tops of the

desks. Therefore the first ten minutes of these tapes are blank.

· An amplifier capable of very loud sound is placed in the office

space at whatever spot is determined to be the most effective.

When the audience enters the office, taped musical arrangements

such as those heard in lobbies and elevators of office buildings

are playing through the amplifier. After ten minutes, the tape

changes to a recording of the typewriting of this scenario.

· The sound of this scenario being typed continues for twenty

minutes, and should end together with the sounds of the portable

tape recorders and those concealed in the desks. But, unlike the

other recorded sounds, the sound of the typing increases gradually

in volume. After fifteen minutes, the sound of typing is

extremely loud, and this volume is maintained for five minutes,

which will seem a very long time.

· The office space will resound like a battlefield. The contact of

a character with paper will sound like the bursting of a shell.
The little pauses for thought while writing the scenario become
huge spaces charged with tense anticipation of the next crash.

- When sound becomes too loud, the body tends to fall asleep.

- Each member of the audience is given two large objects to hold -
a giant pencil and a giant type-writer eraser. As many as are
needed are reproduced from originals made by the author. A set is
placed on the top of each desk, along with 1) a brown Army blanket
and 2) a length of thick rope or a giant version of a rubber band,
before the audience enters the office.

- <u>Cast and Costume</u>

- The following assistants will be needed to perform the piece:

  1) twelve "Secretaries", six male and six female.

  2) two pairs of "Floorwashers", male.

  3) several uncostumed assistants, to handle lighting and sound
     production through the amplifier.

- All the "Secretaries", regardless of size and sex, wear the same
costume - a pair of black men's pants with black suspenders, a
white shirt, and a black and white polka-dot tie. They wear
nothing underneath. The garments are all of the same size. The
pants are 30 inches long in the leg and 36 inches around the
waist. The shirts are 35 inches long in the sleeve and 16 inches
around the neck.

- These are the author's sizes.

- The pockets of the pants are to be filled with small change.

- The "Floorwashers" wear grey coveralls. They carry big mops and

huge buckets of hot smoking water containing a large dose of strong-smelling disinfectant.

- All the assistants wear gym shoes.

- Action

- The audience is kept in a waiting room or a corridor outside the office until preparations are complete. When the first member of the audience enters the office, timing of the piece begins. The office is brightly lit. Soft music is playing. The needed objects are in place on the desks. Each Secretary has chosen a hat tree, and stands by his (her) tree, showing the audience a courteous smile.

- The Floorwashers are aggressively wetting the linoleum. Their action with the mops and water should be directed at the fine shoes of the entering audience members, with the objective of en-couraging them to protect themselves by climbing on the desks. Their doing so will be suggested by the twelve Secretaries, who begin first to demonstrate and then to situate the members of the audience on the desk-tops. Each audience member is covered with the Army blanket and tied with the rope or giant rubber band, around the whole desk. Once tied, they are given the giant pencil and typewriter eraser to hold in their hands.

- The audience is told (not by announcement but quite intimately, by each Secretary) that the giant objects are very fragile and are not to be released. Releasing them would cause them to fall to the floor, to become wet, to be trampled or to be shattered. The audience members can determine with their fingers that the giant objects are indeed very fragile.

- There is no alternative for a decent person and, in the total darkness of the performance, the holding on to the objects may reduce anxiety. The details of the objects may be explored by the fingers as a pass-time.

- The office door is shut. The wall fans spread the stench of heated disinfectant.

- When all the members of the audience are tied in place, the Floor-washers depart with their equipment, not bothering to wipe up any pools of water they have made.

- The Secretaries return to their posts by the trees.

- The fluorescent lamps flicker off, one row after another, leaving the office invisible.

- The soft music played during the positioning of the audience continues for a brief while, then stops abruptly.

- At this moment, the sounds taped on the recorders hidden in the desks should begin, and also the sound of typing carried by the amplifier. At this moment, too, the Secretaries switch on the tape recorders hanging on the hat trees. The Secretaries remove the office costumes, hang them on the trees and strap the oper-ative recorders around their naked waists. They then begin a blind journey through the maze of desks and office equipment, using their hands and feet and other parts of the body to find their way to a hat tree on the opposite side of the office. The trip should take fifteen minutes.

- At the end of the period of large scale typing sound (fifteen

minutes after the lights go out), each Secretary should have found another tree and another costume hanging on the tree. The Secretaries unstrap the recorders, hang them up, and dress again, during the five minute period of silence that follows.

- The absolute darkness continues, but without recorded sound. Members of the audience, adjusting their ears to the new condition, begin to hear the small real sounds in the space. They hear the breathing, coughing and sounds of the others turning and twisting in their uncomfortable positions. They hear the sound of small change in the pockets of the Secretaries' pants as they dress. If suffering from aural overstimulation, they may imagine hearing normally unhearable, miniature sounds, such as the dipping of a tea bag into hot water or the sliding of a metal clip on paper.

- The five minute period of silence ends suddenly with the relighting of the fluorescent lamps. They quiver on; the members of the audience rub their eyes.

- The music resumes where it ended, recalling the moment when a landing plane re-contacts the soothing, sentimental sound that covers the surface of the continent like a natural element. The Secretaries release the audience. The piece is over.

- page 1, left.

- The double-page spread will be a typographical equivalent of the sound, using the words supplied by me (on a typewriter?) It could be black and white or slightly off black or in greys or in colors. It could be overprinted (deep space) or not. The words like line drawings.

- The color photo should show me bound to a desk in a blanket among fifty empty desks in a large room. Alone, or with the 12 secretaries stationed by racks and costumed around the room. A blue-black chrome furniture if no big office is found, just me bound, w. 12 secy's? Hayden?

218

· <u>Theory</u>

· It seems that a long time has passed since the "happenings" of the
early sixties. I ceased using New York settings in 1962 - re-
turning in 1965 for two pieces, but none since then. And since
then only the Massage piece done for Sthlm's Moderna Museet in 66.
I have even used up the audiences on the road and most artlovers
are by now hopelessly overinformed (perhaps) about "happenings" or
maybe not. What I would attempt now with a purity of insistence
on first principles, is the archaeology of the form as I can
remember and put it together from my notes. The audience in this
case may not be surprised, but, participating in a reconstruction
(sort of) may more respect the intentions. - In pieces of the past
many times the audience has resolved a piece out of their surprise
into their own intention - and I have let it go that way because I
couldnt do anything but.

· Lecture form

· A Demonstration is what this perf. is and as appropriate to the
retrospective accounting I am doing, the analysis of self and
work. A demonstration is what its supposed to be, thats the
nature of it, because "happenings" are dead.

· I had left NY originally because I needed new audiences. What
kind of an audience would a demonstration piece require?

· If it is a painting then why not admit that, and not perform it,
simply draw it, or make a model.. photograph specific incidents
which might take place. Set ups. Admit the artificiality of it
all.

219

- Office: a hapg for someone else to do. The first script.

- It is my fantasy anyway why burden the audience unless they will agree to participate in the "construction"?

- This will be a new piece but a model piece, with each step spelled out and documented, and every attempt made to clarify my intentions. My role in this would be more evident, less object-like than usual

- Here I sit, waiting for customers

- Analyst/Private eye

- My happening is not theater - it is more like a painting or sculpt. (a construction) that the "audience" helps compose. Its therefore they feel trapped in what Cage calls a "police" situation. They are taken possession of. Whats required of them is a willingness to let themselves be used, including their emotions as fex. of resistance to being told what to do.

- A perf. is a construction on a large scale arrived at by the appropriation and diversion of found material, using movement, - but very _little_ movement. Performance may be an ironic term.

- Incidents are invented to make the elements of the piece move in certain ways.

- The audience is not liberated (rather, enslaved) nor are they used as individuals. They are parts of the composition.

- If you accept art you accept its authoritarianism. Its a hard question to answer whether art without authority is art or whether art with authority is desirable. The hapng asks questions always, seems to fall inbetween on many issues. An art between authority and license, intention and non-intention.

220

- The aim is the creation of a repeating limited movement, an overall movement, like a machine (characteristic of my perfs.)

- I shd emphasise that a happening is never really about anything
and in that it is like a painting or sculpture which is never
really about anything - except the experience of its creator. I
would not treat the subject - f. ex. the Office - by saying something about the subject. I would use the material of the subject
to arrive at formal effects which wd have various interpretations,
not necessarily having to do with the subject.

- Thousands are lined up to perform the arts of desecration. If it
is form, thats great If it is only form thats not so good and if
it is only madness thats not so good

- happening is art, ie. removal, denial a real orgy is not art

- (art is its own reason for existence. art is not an antagonist to
be removed, like a god or authority, to be shamed & destroyed)

- My hapgs deal with the potentialities of fantasy in a cultural
situation - the manipulation of hidden meanings and small explosions (small things get out). The tension is artistic - ie.
destruction is not the point emotion is the energy that runs the
machine the structure (the machine itself) is religion and art
all my pieces are both religious (magical) and artistic

- That the happening is controlled release of fantasy to do and be
done to...a participation a deflected orgy has always been under-
stood clearly by myself and vaguely by the audience (who complains
about nonparticipation)

- sometimes the audience is used just as witness

- Concern w. the American psyche rather than politics....

- The sixties were a period when the American psyche was split open like Pandora's Box and its self-destructive fantasy released. The happenings at the beginning of the decade were at once a symptom of this and an attempt to turn the cruel forces, directed at one-self and others into form. In countries where revolution was more the issue, happenings became the abuse of order, disruption for it its own sake. But the American problem remains the schizoid psyche and its reeling from one extreme to another, from puritanism to abandon, from solicitude to aggression. My happenings sought as I say both to excite and to sublimate the dangerous forces, and aimed at art, a value of order which I maintain arbitrarily, and for its own sake, which is to say the essence of shape and organization.

- In the second stage of preparation which is preparation not alone but _with_ and _among others_ - called "rehearsal" which is not a rehearsal but a ranging over the site and development of individual fantasy and interest with the details of the site in terms of the material of the site. Followed by a selection combining alone thoughts and thoughts with others alone events and events with others into an operational script - instructions of a practical sort

- The final result gives a sense of satisfaction both as a whole & to the individuals involved (or should). If the individuals in a piece feel bossed around by me or anyone else, its because a gap

in the consistency has had to be filled They didnt provide the
business they were expected to provide

· I stoke emotion all participants are engaged in the forming of
desire into substitutes, that's accepted. In their intellectual
approach the pieces could be said to be psychoanalytical

· motive and construction a model of a work of art's origins,
inspiration, functioning (machine of art)

· Doing a hapng is finding my way back difficultly to my basic behavior Hence this awful preliminary subjectivity and the strain..

· All the above results from my trying to locate "my" theater in my
compulsions. An "honest" theater. Just a theater of myself..
These are the impulses. I can still say that form is the end and
that interpretation of the results is divergent and rich (by
others as well as myself)

· I am not able to break thru into reality, to do my fantasies.
Hapgs project them most realistically, more than a dream but still
they are fantasy.

· They may start with a real place but it is the use by my fantasy
of that place that is the final result.. They reflect my tension

· Psychological expressionism That why its so foolish to compare my
hpgs with Cages or others I pursue them to the "honest" subject,
which makes the sweat break out The difficulty of realizing a
fantasy even in a removed way is tremendous. Punishment by
confession.

They are psychological a thing an obstacle, not a thing to see
through

223

- Happening consists of the acting out in fantasy of cruel acts imagined by me. "Its only theater".

- It includes fetishism (objects) A theater of objects. Only I know what I am acting out (?).

- It includes masochism. I hide myself, I disguise myself a beggar. I dirty myself etc.

- Self-punishment by confession.

- My hapngs only touch me if they do take a cruel turn. Beginning a happening I have to pass through rationalizations

- Police procedures cruel acts against the audience are part of my style To be cruel or to hurt

- Universalized thru a common cultural bond, clothes fex. (Moms of a period), and deliberately typicalized by study of magazines. My fetish collection tends to be <u>pictures of</u>..rather than things themselves. The early hapng treated woman as victim. This I wouldnt want to do now - secy model or what, I would try to treat them as people, let them develop their own role, not forgetting they may want to be treated as victims. But a seeing of <u>them</u> rather than an abstraction of fantasy

- I know the artists ways (my ways) I handle (?) my madness

- The artist is a lunatic authoritarian and sadist and he must <u>go</u> (self destruction)

- Esq. should have mentioned this in their issue but the liberal mind would not recognize this.

- The artist visual is a fantast the happening is the test of his fantasy against reality it is anti-studio

224

- Artist is archaic or so I feel myself to be It is a matter of definition (?) Or is definition archaic
- Elimination of the visual - trend of the final part of the sixties
- When the sound element.... my next step in perfs was taken away, what was I left with, the old stuff
- I got into a project much too large here as a result of the emphasis on the visual - because of the page medium a silent one. My original idea was for a sound happeng since I am particularly tuned to sound just now, in darkness, but of course thats impossible. That would have been simpler to prepare.
- What about a page of black or very near brown black or a double-page spread with reverse lettering, descriptions of sounds?
- I <u>blockade</u> the force towards union to create tension which is as much an aim in my theater as eventual satisfaction.
- The tension of simultaneous satisfactions.
- as in Moviehouse, the satisfaction of sitting down, even the health of it, was blockaded, by art (an order) - but sitting down accomplished nothing but resting yr. weary bones.
- the naked bodies used as tension not for freedom - something one wants to see
- nudity is cultural material.
- Adaptability is the sense stimulated by the happenings as I do them, invention, substitution, taking advantage of situation. This is why the effect of a happening is felt as a participation and less as a spectacle being observed. With an audience, the extension of participation is always intended, if not always

realized. A brutal provocation may be a reverse invitation.

Involving an audience is not an easy matter. I prefer small

audiences, no larger than 50, and such an audience may be con-

sidered members of a cast, somewhat removed. A larger audience,

even 200, is a herd, an other object entirely. Brutalization of

such a number does not turn into invitation but brutal response.

- I reach audiences (the size that can be reached) not by talking

to them but by creating conditions for their bodies which join

them materially to the "performers" and "performance". Enclosure,

darkness, activation of space by increase of moisture or other

particles (dust, talcum), all-over sound, etc. In the Typewriter,

the audience is tied to the environment, and very vulnerable

physically. Fear unites an audience (in the Typewriter, silent

period, they will listen for the small sounds of other members of

the audience).

Seance

Putting audiences to sleep more or less is what Ive been doing for

years. Lately I have been putting them into reclining positions.

- The passion for oneness union is an accepted thing, that bodies

seek back to bodies. If one stands back a bit, its rather bizarre

but its understandable, almost a natural law. The solid state.

I dont know myself whether its a value or an irresistible force.

- I like to accept definitions completely, literally, which usually

means going to extremes.

- Theres nothing unified about sexual union, not for the two or

more involved or and not for the observers. But if a theater

space is <u>solid</u> there is union. If a theater space is open with
individuals walking about in it, there is no unity.

· Sex is one of many actions. The identification thru material
sensation and imagination of bodies as a body, in a body, is the
more profound sense of union.

· Face the dissatisfying fact that this archaeology will necessarily
seem very subjective, more than the result if the hapng preparation had gone through the contact with others to a conclusion of
actual performance. I prepare within myself a setting to operate
from, which is much altered and redefined by contact with actual
events and other persons.

· This archaeology strictly speaking is only half the whole matter.
It ends on a note of uncertainty. Though the scenario has been
imagined to pretty complete definition, it would no doubt change
when tried in a real situation. The contact with reality was
brief and painful, at the office. We did not stay to resolve the
wound we made in the office into form. We left behind us dissat-
isfaction and absence of definition

· The test or the making of a piece is in putting it into action.
The scenario here is more complete than most having been imagined
through several times, but it wd still be subject to change in
practise

· I must stress that the happening is invention out of action and
response to situation. The scenario is literally a pretext, a
provocation, sometimes an outrage, which a cast & individuals deal
with culturally and from a survival point of view. I also know

how inappropriate one persons scenario is to anothers. The
resistance and conflict reshapes the action.

Annotations by the Author

STARS

23 : 15   Jim Dine's happenings
23 : 23   a salesman's spiel in a Washington dime store
23 : 24   *(hes.)* — hesitation, pause
24 : 8   record by Esther Phillips, used in the performance
24 : 13   another record used in the performance
24 : 14   "I Will Follow You", record
24 : 18   *greeng* — Green gallery
           Lex. Hall — Lexington Hall, University of Chicago, site of
           happening GAYETY in 1963
24 : 25   another record used in the performance
26 : 13   *BLT.* — bacon, lettuce, and tomato sandwich
26 : 15   *(5fl.)* — 5th floor
28 : 24   *quick come-to-lifes* — performers 'frozen' in positions, like statues,
           briefly come to life then 'freeze' again
29 : 11   *record cab calls* — the sounds of the two-way radio heard in
           taxi cabs
32 : 18   *Cleaners* — performers who sprayed air purifier between events
32 : 20   transparencies of Washington sights, altered by coloring, pasting,
           piercing etc., projected during the performance
37 : 4   posters announcing the performance
37 : 20   *th.* — theater
39 : 20   construction based on a sewn 'Wheaties' cereal box, used in the
           performance
43 : 18   like the giant bacon, lettuce, and tomato sandwich (BLT) shown at
           the same time in the "Popular Images" exhibition (see 8 : 18)
47 : 16   *W.G. of M.A.* — Washington Gallery of Modern Art
50 : 3   *R + R* — Rock and Roll

MOVEYHOUSE

54 : 1   *SKISS* — Swed. — sketch; i.e.: sketch number one
54 : 11   The events were advertised as 'expanded cinema'
54 : 14   The performance eventually took place at the 41st St. Theater
55 : 8   *dom* or *Dom* — Dominic Capobianco, a performer
55 : 25   Helene Faison, who did not join the cast
56 : 24   heroine of the Film "King Kong"
56 : 25   heroine of "Typee" by Herman Melville
57 : 2   France Raysse, a performer. Since she did not speak English, her
           instruction cards had to be translated into French
57 : 8   as when trying to calm the audience in the face of disaster
58 : 18   Frannie Breer, who did not join the cast
59 : 15   *sp. eff.* — special effects
61 : 24   *Tsq film* — Times Square film. 8 mm film of stripper removing her
           clothes. "Lizard battle" — silent 8 mm film of the battle of lizards
           sequence from "1 000 000 B.C."
62 : 16   pink rubber balls used on the streets of New York
68 : 1   final program

80 : 3   Rudolph Wurlitzer
81 : 2   A fan was placed in front of the projector, to exaggerate the flicker
           effect
81 : 5   *inspoturition* — inspiration plus spot (light) and also perhaps intuition;
           parturition; happy coincidence. The wheels of the bicycle carried in
           the beam of the spotlight revolved also, but more slowly than the
           blades of the fan, located in front of the projector.
81 : 8   fan = projector = cycle = circle
81 : 11   *Oats, (Peas), Beans* — a children's song played during the
           performance by Liz Stevens de Blanc
81 : 12   *Academy of Music* — film theater on 14th Street, New York
81 : 25   Marvelous constructions are built only to be filmed.
           In MOVEYHOUSE, on the contrary, the film is merely the occasion
           for an appreciation of the real events. There was no film in the
           projector during the performance.
82 : 8   To use a thing inappropriately in order to focus attention on the
           thing for its own sake, apart from its function
82 : 11   *Fan - devil* — in Swedish, Fan means Devil
82 : 12   *Fan Tan* — was a brand of chewing gum; *mug* — "Mug", the title
           of a sculpture I made in 1960
83 : 8   the first model of the Fan subject was built about the same
           time as the performance
84 : 2   later "Mouse Museum"
84 : 3   i.e.: not used in advertising the performance
84 : 12   Dick Higgins
84 : 18   *spawn* — the many happening-type performances then being done
85 : 7   Billy Klüver
86 : 4   from the "Village Voice", spring 1966

The material on pp. 82 — 87 was written later, in the spring and early summer
of 1966

MASSAGE

89 : 1   Swed. — notes on arrival!
89 : 9   Swed. — give me the zebra!
89 : 10   Swed. — come with me Stina...we'll row to China...the ark will
           rock...a rowboat is fast enough... From the Swedish version
           of the popular song "Slow Boat to China"
89 : 13   Swed. — the year of the "Third Man" ... I saw the film seven
           times ... Three times since then
89 : 16   *warm korv*; correctly: varm korv. A steamed sausage sold on the
           streets in Stockholm
           (I hand) — in hand
90 : 2   *RÖSTA MJUK* — vote soft; *(ÅKE MJUK)* — suggested name of
           candidate for a soft party
90 : 7   *SUCK* — sigh

90 : 8   *PRICK* — dot

90 : 9   *FART* — speed

90 : 10   Swed. — a crooked copyist roasts a grape. Nonsense phrase composed
          for the sake of its sound. RUNKRÖKT; correctly: Rundkrökt

91 : 3   The first formulation was a performance to take place aboard a ship
          in Stockholm harbor. It was abandoned because it was too difficult
          to arrange. Instead, the objects in my exhibition at the Moderna
          Museet were moved aside and the performance took place there.

91 : 10   Swed. — "Amok is a Malayan word which means rage, a fury so
          violent in an individual that he wishes his own destruction — but at
          the same time wants to take as many people as possible with him
          into the grave.
          A recent illustration: the student who spread death and terror from
          the tower at the University in Austin, Texas, some months ago.
          We have in Sweden in modern times had two such amok-runners,
          and today I shall tell about the first one who, one day in May 1900,
          inscribed his name on one of the darkest pages of our history
          of crime.
          Even if today there are not many who have an immediate memory
          of the murder orgy, there are certainly many who have heard from
          their parents about Johan Filip Nordlund, 'the wild beast on the
          Prins Carl'.
          A tall man in a blue raincoat
          While the amok-runners of the East act in blind rage, it seems as if
          their counterparts in the West are psychically strong enough to plan
          their crimes quite carefully. But not even they know anything of
          their future victims; they strike whoever comes in their way.
          Another common feature is that the perpetrator usually does not
          show any sign of mental illness in advance. On the contrary, they
          may be friendly, calm individuals who suddenly are seized by
          madness.
          No one at the small hotel in Köping thought that the guest, 'Mr.
          Grönqvist', behaved strangely, though the tall, slim man in the
          dark blue raincoat did not seem to have any special business in the
          small town on Lake Mälar. He often went out on walks and on
          May 17th he walked towards the harbor, where the white ship
          Prins Carl was scheduled to leave for Stockholm that same evening.
          Perhaps the ship officers thought there was something a bit unusual
          about the stranger who went aboard several times during the day,
          peering into various spaces....."

91 : 24   Swed. — on the white ship

92 : 12   *Tub* — tube

92 : 15   *Kar* — tub (the Swedish word for man is karl, pronounced kar)
          BADKAR — bathtub

92 : 16   *SKROV* — hulk

92 : 19   *ANIARA* — a Swedish opera which takes place on board a space
          ship

92 : 21   *OMBORD* — aboard. Also: om — about; bord — table

93 : 16   Swed. — "A strange man in a long blue raincoat went aboard the
          Mälar-ship Prins Carl in Köping in the year 1900. A few hours

later, he had tried to kill everyone on board. The murderer is still
an enigma. Was he mentally deranged?"

93 : 23   In Sweden, a name is assigned to each day. As a matter of fact, Carl
is *not* my name day, though I was born on that day.

93 : 24   In fact Nordlund was *not* a friend of my maternal grandfather, Thure,
who became in later years a physical therapist, practising the
Ling system of massage.

93 : 25   The year of my mother's birth was 1900

93 : 26   Pontus Hultén, the director of the Moderna Museet, told me that
he owns the embalmed triggerfinger of Nordlund.

95 : 9   Swed. — "A MADMAN IS LOOSE ON BOARD!"

96 : 7   *SILL* — herring

97 : 19   *björn* — bear. *Nalle, bearboo* — pet names for bear

97 : 20   *hjortron* — cloudberries

97 : 21   *mors lilla* — mother's little. First words of a children's song about a
boy, Olle, who encounters a bear while picking blueberries

99 : 2   *Rbergs goat* — Rauschenberg's construction "Monogram", owned
by the Moderna Museet, which includes a stuffed goat

99 : 7   Öyvind Fahlström

99 : 25   *(Nissefex)* — Nisse, for example. Nisse — first name of the chief
caretaker of the museum

100 : 8   *biologisk museet*; correctly: biologiska — The Museum of Natural
History

100 : 15   large painted representations of food, made for a dance concert
in 1961, became a *prefiguration* of large objects made the
following year

101 : 22   *KROPPKAKA* — potato pastry. *KROPP* — body. *KAKA* — cake

101 : 24   Swed. — in the museum cloakroom and elsewhere

102 : 6   *cocobollar* — coconut covered candy in ball form

102 : 9   *städning* — cleaning up, setting things in order

102 : 10   *sparkboll* — soccer ball

102 : 11   *ALLKOPIA* — a photocopy firm

102 : 24   *hängmatta* — hammock

103 : 2   *Klister* — Library paste

103 : 3   dedicated to Oscar Andersson (1877-1906) Swedish caricaturist

103 : 5   *älskling* — darling

103 : 6   Swed. — "what's going on there?"

103 : 12   *Handelsbanken* — prestigious bank in Stockholm with large
windows suitable for a performance

103 : 25   *PORR* — Swedish slang for pornography

104 : 3   *MATSAL* — dining room

104 : 20   *GE* — give. *TING* — thing. Geting — wasp

105 : 20   *(konst)* — (art)

105 : 23   *skjut + drag* — push + pull

106 : 3   Swed. — keep nature clean

106 : 10   Swed. — "Novels about doctors in pocketbook format
The White Series
Nurse Tanya at war
Once again Glen Carew operated at the front. "

107 : 11   Masse — assistant caretaker of the museum

107 : 24   *Syster Mia* — my nanny
107 : 25   *L.holmen* Långholmen — Long Island, island near Stockholm,
           site of several monument proposals
    : 1   Staffan Olzon, filmmaker and playwright
 1   : 23   *Storkyrkan* — "The Great Church", in Stockholm's old city
109 : 18   *Matt piska*; correctly: mattpiska — rug beater
110 : 18   *ide* — lair, den; place of hibernation
111 : 4   During the preparation of the performances a sensational murder
           occured in the city in which a man was beaten to death with a
           typewriter.
111 : 6   make copies of three Picasso sculptures outside the museum for
           every performance
111 : 7   *K bröd* — Knäckebröd, crisp brown rye bread
111 : 10   *SÖNDAGS–NISSE STRIX* — "The Sunday Gnome–Owl", a
           Swedish humor magazine
111 : 15   George Denny (Denney Jr.), husband of Alice D. of Washington,
           D.C. In 1963, he stopped the record player at a party for artists by
           pulling out the plug.
112 : 22   *hölass* — a wagon full of hay
113 : 1   *M.M.*; abbreviation for the Swedish equivalent for 'etc'.
113 : 2   Swed. — Composition for a cloakroom with coats, a stairway, a few
                   rooms, some doors, spectators, etc.
                   by Claes Oldenburg
                   (a happening)
113 : 10   *i stiltje* — dead calm
113 : 15   Swed. — disrobing
                   exercise
                   repose (with a dream)
113 : 24   *pytt i panna* — dish of fried egg over diced meat
114 : 5   *SIX MAIX* — name of woman participating in performance
114 : 8   *Hylla* — shelf. The part of the Museum above the cloakroom is
           nicknamed 'Hyllan' — the shelf.
114 : 10   *sängdags* — bedtime
114 : 16   *med hjälp av* — assisted by
115 : 3   Swed. — some others who assist by reclining and spectators who in
           due time also recline
115 : 11   *Djur* — animal
115 : 12   *svamp* — mushroom
           Sköterska — nurse
115 : 13   *Massör* — masseur
115 : 15   *Sovande* — sleeper
115 : 16   *Brevbärare* — postman
115 : 23   *generalrepetition* — dress rehearsal
118 : 10   *sitt ej i stolarna* — no seating
118 : 18   *SÅ–INTE SÅ* — this way — not that way
           The caption for a cartoon sequence called "The Art of Sitting" by
           Oscar Andersson.
119 : 5   drawing of a round wooden tub which in Swedish is 'så'.
           P planes — the Picasso sculpture is an enlargement in
           concrete of drawings on cardboard and therefore flat.
           or *(biolog museum)* — something resembling the installation at

THE TYPEWRITER

Examples of the Original Manuscript

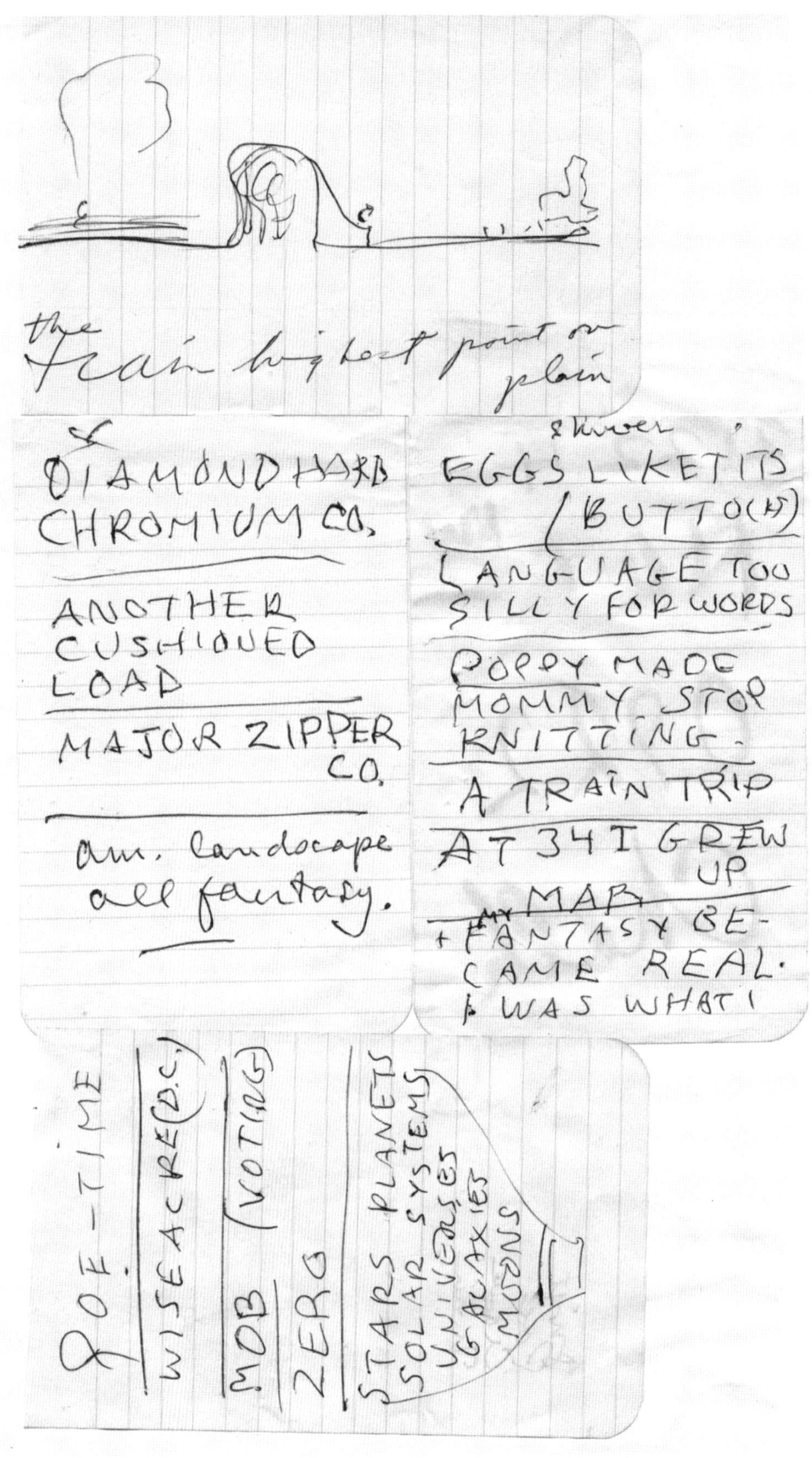
the
Train highest point on
plain

DIAMONDHARD
CHROMIUM CO.

ANOTHER
CUSHIONED
LOAD

MAJOR ZIPPER
CO.

Am. landscape
all fantasy.

skiver
EGGS LIKE TITS
(BUTTON)

LANGUAGE TOO
SILLY FOR WORDS

POPPY MADE
MOMMY STOP
KNITTING.

A TRAIN TRIP

AT 34 I GREW
UP
MAB
+ FANTASY BE-
CAME REAL.
I WAS WHAT I

POE - TIME

WISEACRE (D.C.)

MOB (VOTING)

ZERO

STARS PLANETS
SOLAR SYSTEMS
UNIVERSES
GALAXIES
MOONS

PREVIOUSLY I
(I THOUGHT) WAS.
ONLY

THE DREAM.

A SHORT STORY
in my inexcusable

SOMEONE TAKES
NOTES — READS
THEM.

DEER FOUNDRY
FISHMAN WOOL
PULLERS
DYE WORKS.

POE — R. GRILLET
CAOUTCHOUC

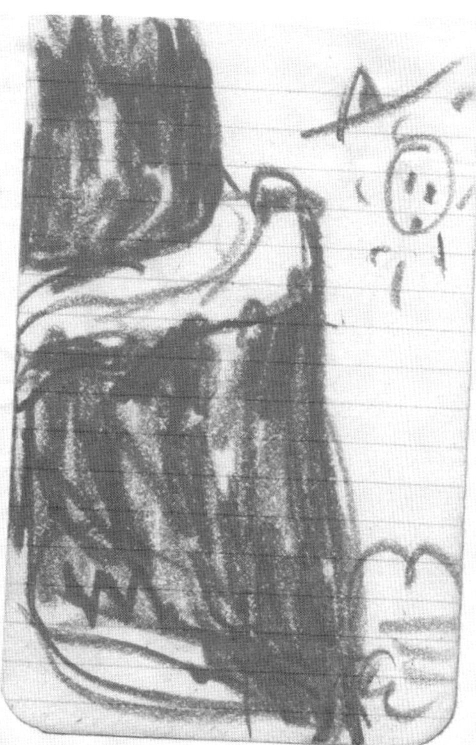

COLUMBIA 5-3612

Mr. Beal or Mrs. Oliphant

**CAFETERIA AND RESTAURANT WORKERS
UNION LOCAL 473, AFL-CIO**

OLIVER T. PALMER
BUSINESS AGENT

1438 YOU STREET N.W.
WASHINGTON, D. C.

Eric W
336 Dent Pl
NW
Wash 7.

Vogue
1438 U NW
Mr. Jacobs. 05-3612
Willard Banquet.
500   P & 14 St
Crystal NA 8-4420
Dance 210. Tued Thu.
Majestic
1632 U NW

Ghoundbus
1110 NY av NW

egg roll

New Weston. NY.
Jacobsen Teaching B-more
Cairo — HO 2-2104
gally 66.7-5221

AUTOS
INITIALS
CLEANING

Central 9 — D+E
Rocket R+R
          12 +NY
Starlite 149+irv
Champagne 13+F

POSTERS

program
statement
pink sheets
+ 1,
    2. cast-names

capitol
was mass
+ all rolled
off roller;
as shirt
as suit
eh.

CLEANERS

STAR RUG WORKS.
        P ST

The very
inelusible
single
word.
      NOT JUST
      CUTE

INSTITUTE FOR
DEAF
SOUSA (BRIDGE)

Baltimore is
never seen either
by train or car
because of tunnels.

PAT BLOX
WC Fields

greensburg,
red devil
red + green
lights

GUILT — DICK
DICKIE

*STARRCARPETWORKS

BELLAMY

maine ave
philip stern +
julian plays
squash.
HANDBALL
SQUASH

UNIVERSAL
SCHOOL
OF TRUTH
670916 NW

gyms 3825 friends school
univ are

skating rink
Arena on wheels
47th Kaleorama
NO 72465

Western high
sch.

gtown.
35 + Kenmore

gtown Univ. gym.

America Univ.

GW 21 + H
HOW 24006
Am MASS +
NEB
gro 37 + 0

HAWAIIAN
BEAUTY
PORO BEAUTY SCHOOL
Barber Sch.
LAWANDA SCH OF
BEAUTY CULTURE

DRY CLEANERS
+
DYERS
WET WASH

LAUNDRY [FOAM

(89¢) SHIRTS, SUITS

(Austo)

cleaners. red
+
white

red cleaners signs

SPECIAL

machinery factory.

WHITE-
FACTORY
LAUNDRY.
steam.
hoses-
ir. board.

negroes in rela-
tion to white-
thru laundry.
cleaners.

place poster.

five shows make

P C. Sam.
Dan.

Ex. Kelly
965-1746

Fox etc

flamingo
( ) WASH

Red dress cairo bag | MUST BE FORMAL BASIS

ring
312 W
29 ,
X

"money made in mint.
water runs down side pan eyes.

bus backs in bugle call scrunches.

SPRING
at
HOME
MILITARY
POLITICAL

plane flying over

from Bascent.

Camel TEST

PILOT

people seated around on benches — party game
— 2 birds —
etc.

MUSIC.
Bird calls — pigeon crows
mourning doves
Bicycles
planes.

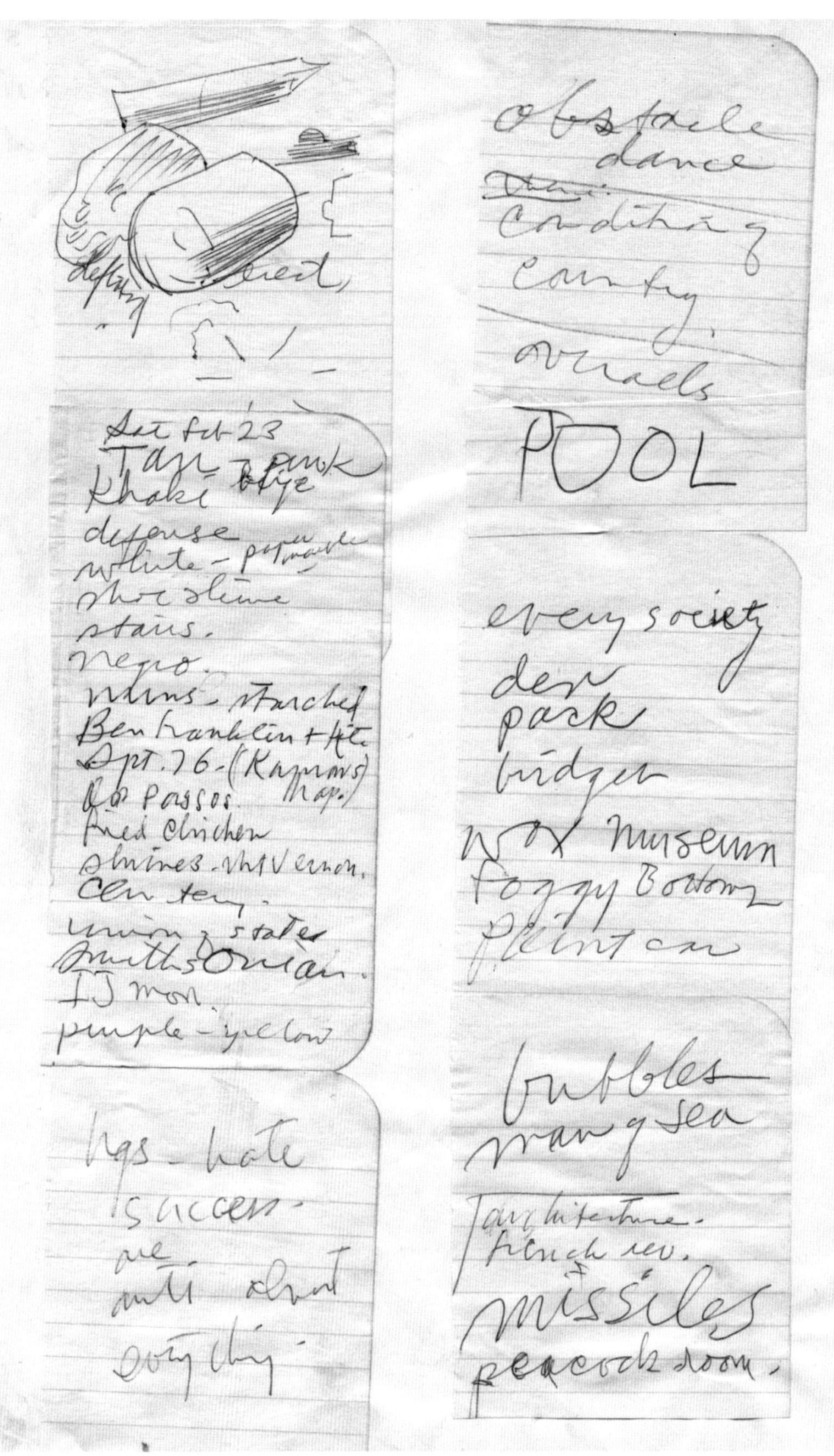
defiang tired,

Sat Feb 23
Tan — pink
khaki — olive
defense
white — pop made
shoe shine
stairs.
negro.
nuns — starched
Ben Franklin + kite
Spt. 76 — (Kaprow's nap.)
Dos Passos.
fried chicken
shrines. Mt Vernon.
cemetery.
union station
Smithsonian.
I J Mon
purple — yellow

has — hate
is success —
ive
until about
every thing.

obstacle
dance
conditioning
country.
overalls.
POOL

every society
den
pack
budget
Wax museum
Foggy Bottom
Clinton

bubbles
wan of sea
architecture.
french rev.
missiles
peacock room.

Margot + Faut.
Underpass X
M street
cabana
aunt gull.
market
garage X
Boat Club
Va.

J. F. K.
R. V. S. P.
V. I. P.
R. I. P.
D. A. R.
AAAAAA

flour
cement
baffles

old market

patriotic
paraphernalia

parties
hostess
invites.

INITIALS =
POWER

F D R
FeDeRal

POWER (NOT MONEY)

afraid
of
bulls

Templeton
house.
sun up.

back
drop
garden
pulled
up

Sunken
Mt Vernon,

White Swan

JAPAN trees

crabs clams,
oysters.

DU PONT
Underpass

sunken boat

lemon yellow
white
black.

HE SITS

stars are
lites in dark
~~in~~ in which
one may read
an
arrangement.

are conveyances
are radiations
(streets)
are cemeteries
are birds.

Baseball

stars

more

stars.

WASH ST.

O circles

Stars

banquet.

Emilio
Pit'

girl tattoo.

symbols.

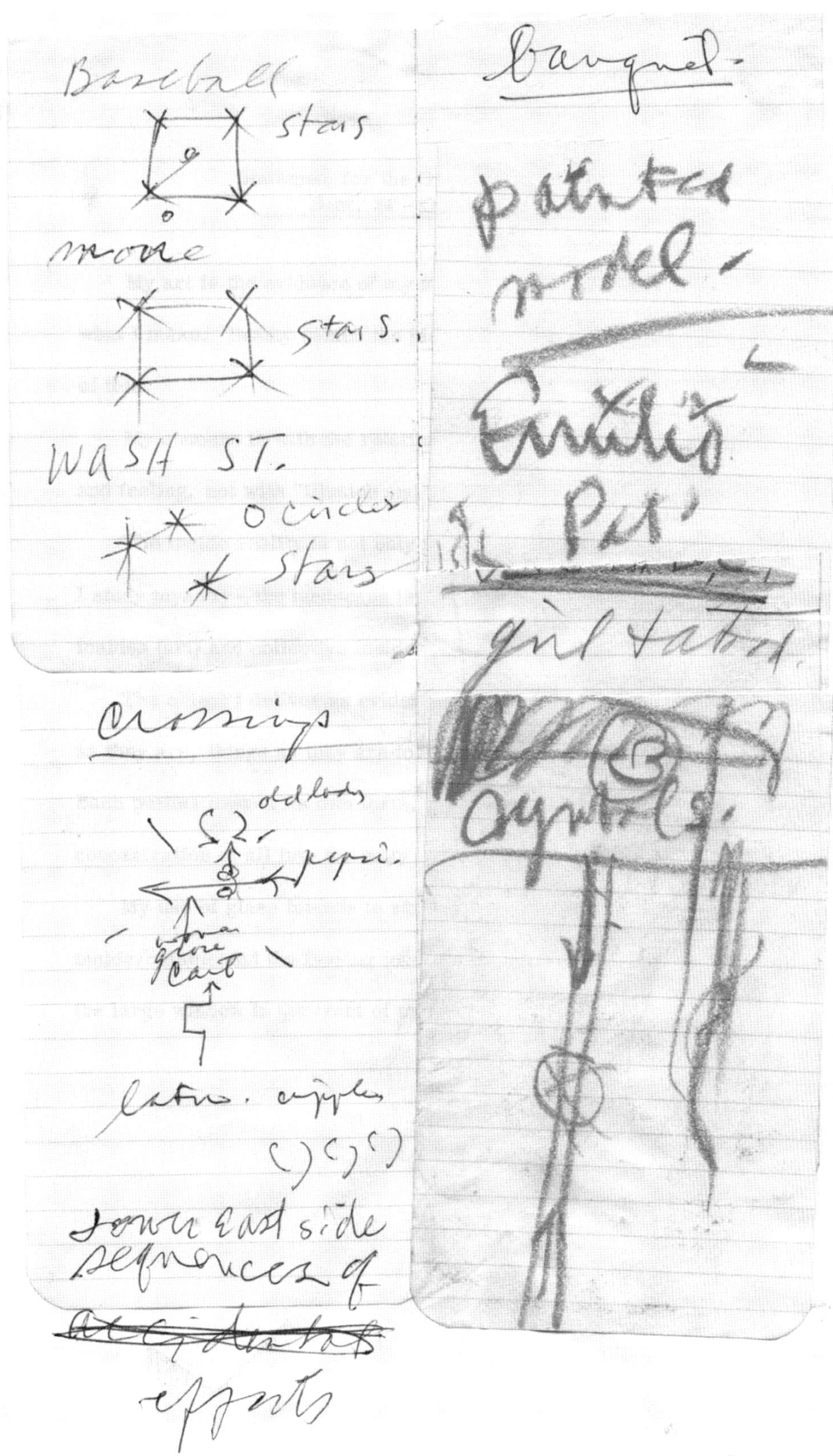

crossings

old lady

pupil.

Latin. nipples

( ) ( ) ( )

Lower East Side
sequences of

efforts

X

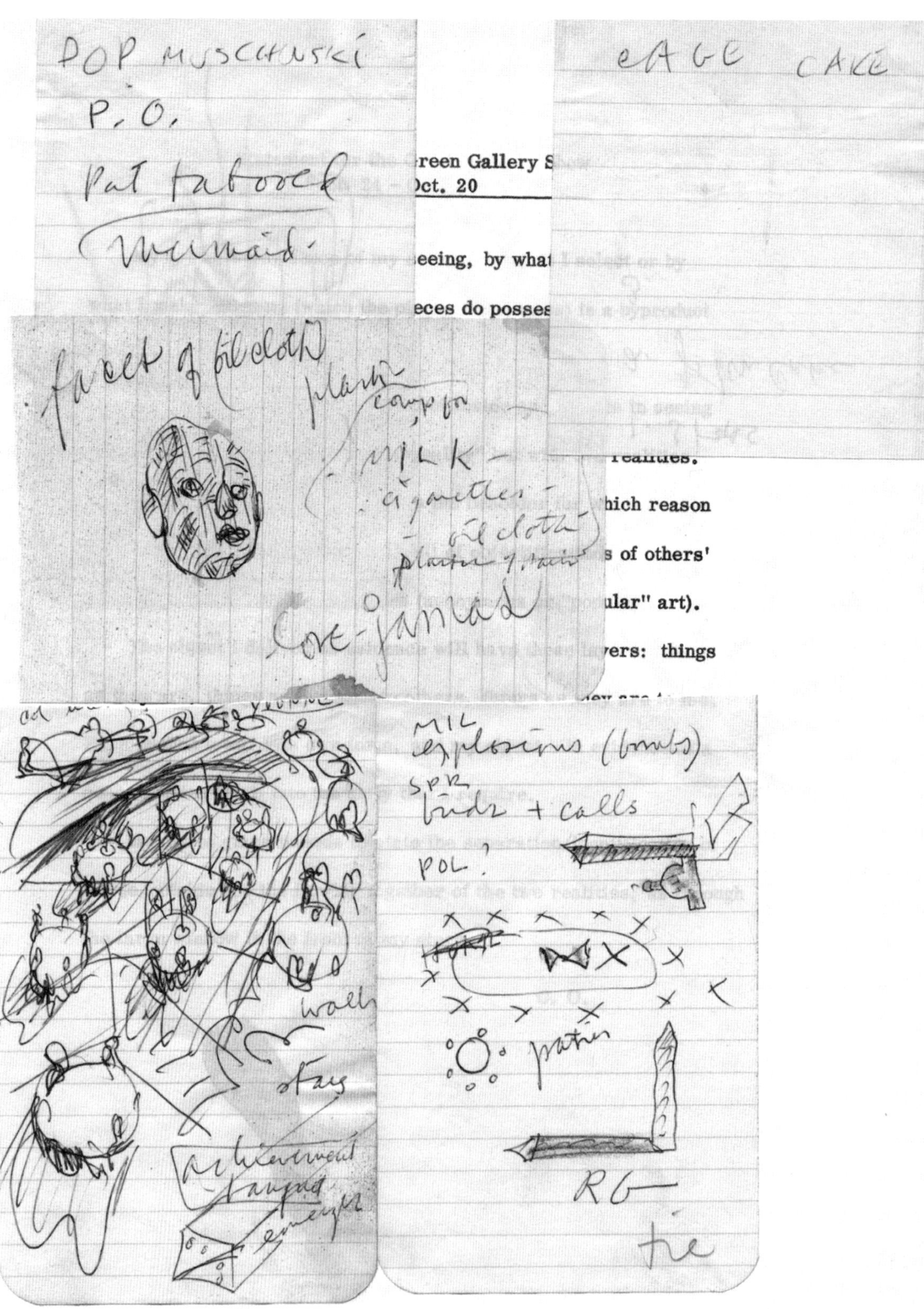
POP MYSCHINSKI
P.O.
Pat tabook
mermaid
eAGE CAKE
reen Gallery
Oct. 20
facet of oilcloth
MILK
cigarettes
oil cloth
Cort-jamad
MIL
explosions (bombs)
birds + calls
POL?
walls
stars
achievement
langue
emerge
RG
he

1. anno.
2. res. for series
   calendar.
3. ~~catalog~~ press
              release
4. catalog

members. 5. whole
onwids 10. whole

1. Cast
   lecture   19 apr.
5. filmn   23 may
2. typg   24, 25
3 dance   9 may
4 lecture   16 may
            reassembl
nous june 2

Record
Cat
Calls.

WASHINGTON

whites
+
browns.

(MILITARY.
  NEGRIES
  POTOMAC

$24 = 6$

$25 = 7$

$26 = 8$

Initials!

secretaries

all great
great notions
at last clean
down to what
can be done + it
is right A.

classic
cleaners
classic
                white
clean = right
clean design —
          flag.
          emblem
          wash jtg.
flag = clothes =
      tablecloths
peau b (ie) (ee) st.

Op. dot

Vlaspol Hahn

3022 Gov. Tan.

Bird

Calls

(Spring)

Reservations

Sybil Meyersburg
Dr Meyersburg

Cherry B
time,
April 8 – ?

Doria Higgins
Apt J-2-B
University Apts.
Durham, N.C.

McKinney
Helene Herzbrun
American University
Art Dept. WO 6-6890
X 262

Ft. McNair
Oyster.

X

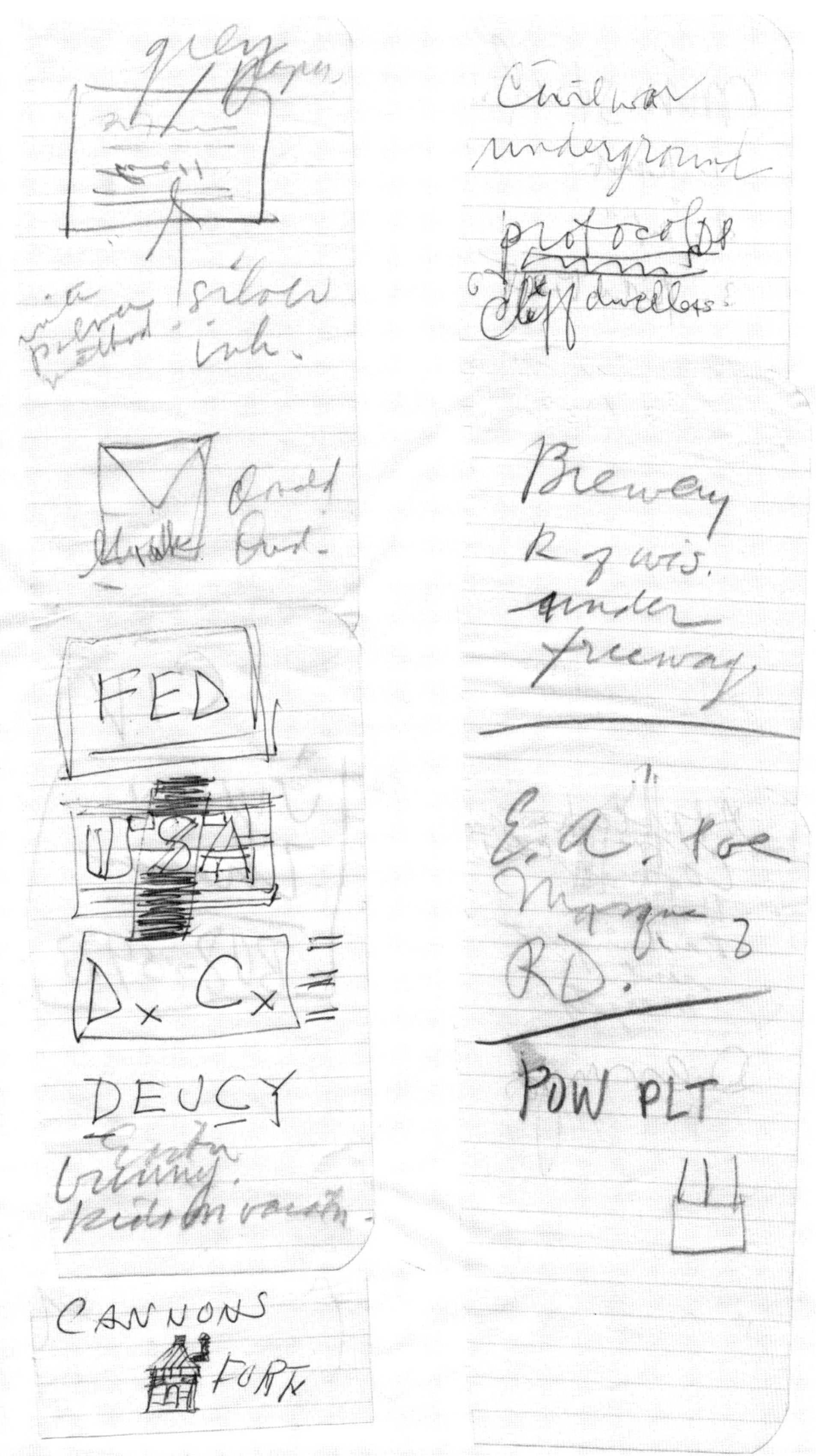
grey paper
silver ink.
Civil war
underground
protocols
cliff dwellers.
Red
Cx
Brewery
R of wis.
under
freeway
FED
USA
D x   C x
DEUCY
E. A. Poe
Masque
R.D.
POW PLT
CANNONS
FORT

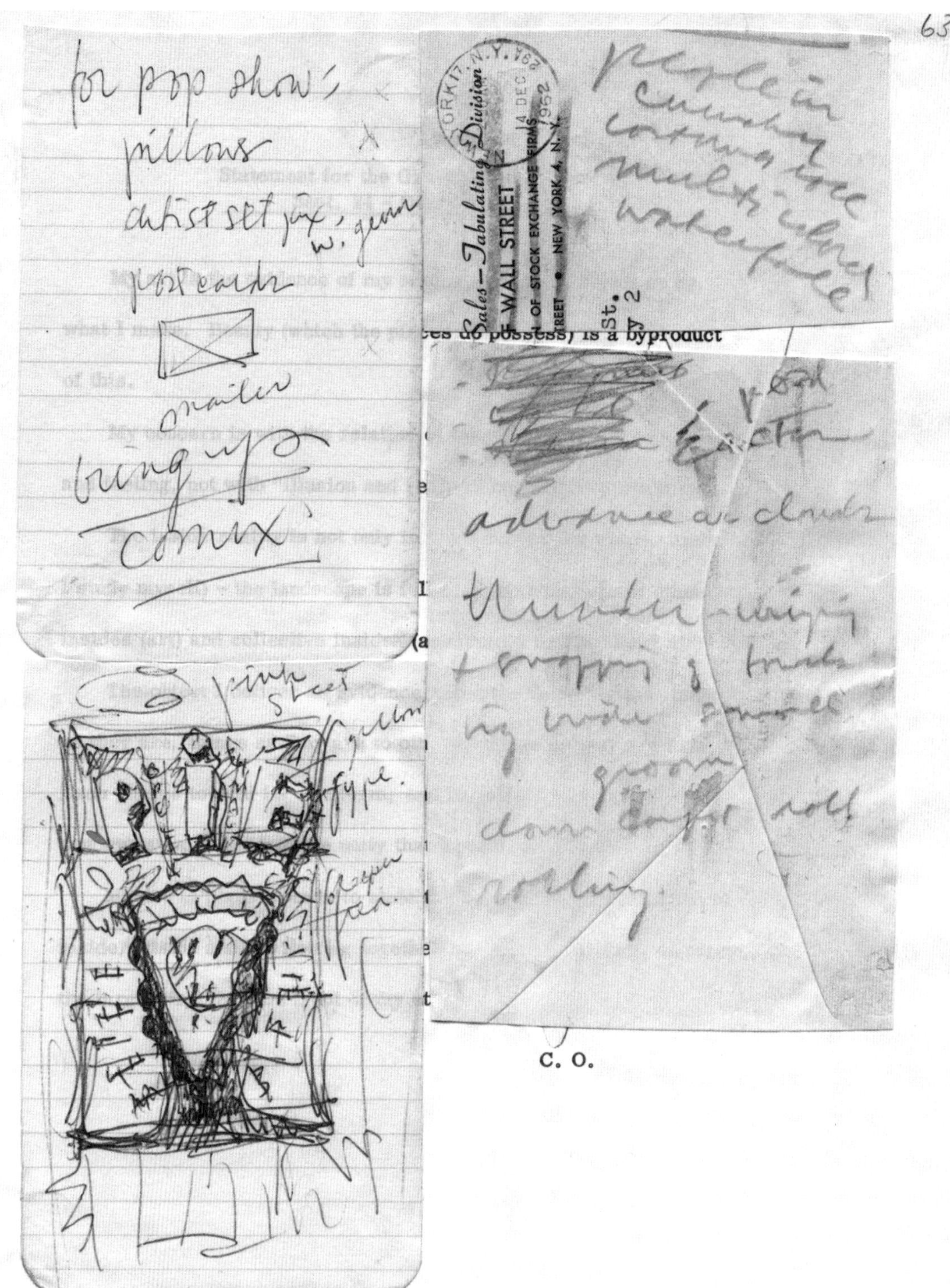

for pop show:
pillows
artist set jar, w. germ
postcard
mailer
bring up
comix

c. o.

RAY GUN MAP #3

CLEANERS*

WASHINGTON, D.C.

* ARISTO CLEANERS - P. ST + 21. ST NW - SUITS 89¢
SHIRTS

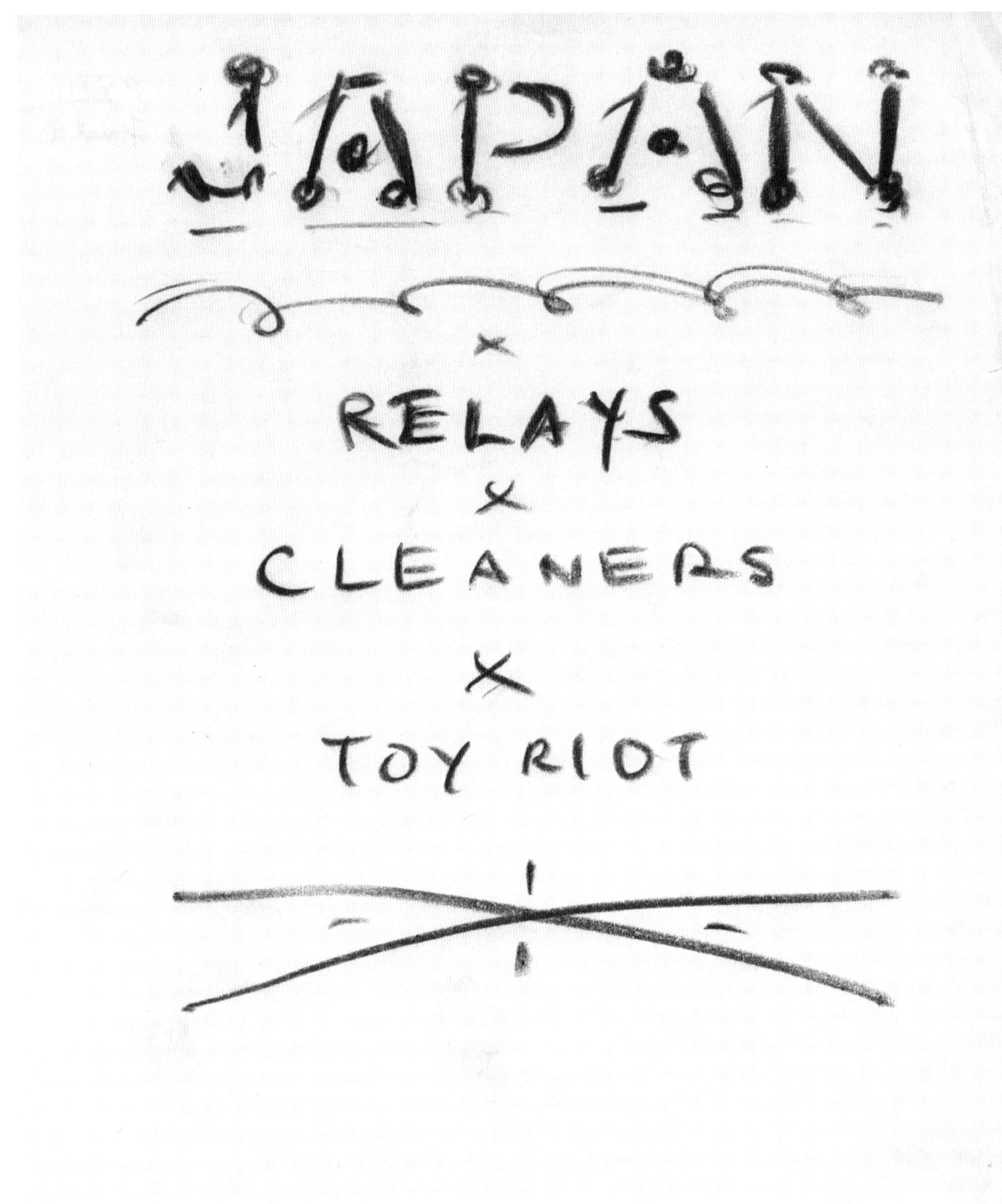

Sketch for a poster

Sketch for a poster

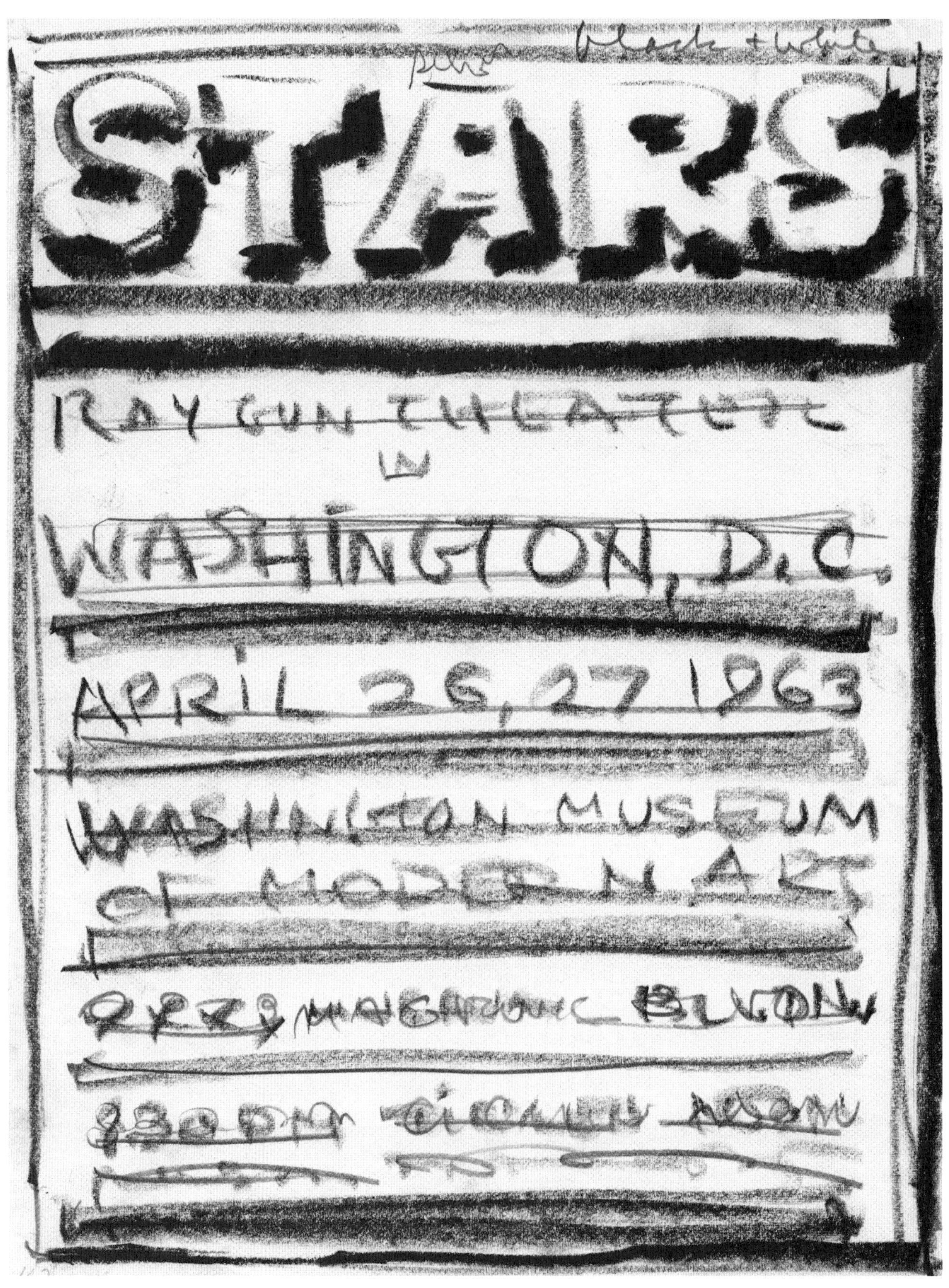

Sketch for a poster

STARS

A Farce for Objects

April 24, 25, 1963

8:30 P.M.

By

Claes Oldenburg

Players

Olga Adorno	Gail Hillow
Thomas Bartlett	Ed Kelley
Cathleen Bingham	Charles Lilly
Michael Booth	Joan Mason
Gil Carter	Pat Oldenburg
Chris Denney	Alan Raywid
Jill Denney	Bette Rickerson
Joan Fugazzi	Thomas Roberts
Fred Goldfrank	Cindy Warren
Gloria Graves	Clarence Wheat
Chris Harris	

-- The piece lasts 48 minutes --

Commissioned by the

WASHINGTON GALLERY OF MODERN ART

At the Gallery

Made in Washington, D.C., U.S.A.

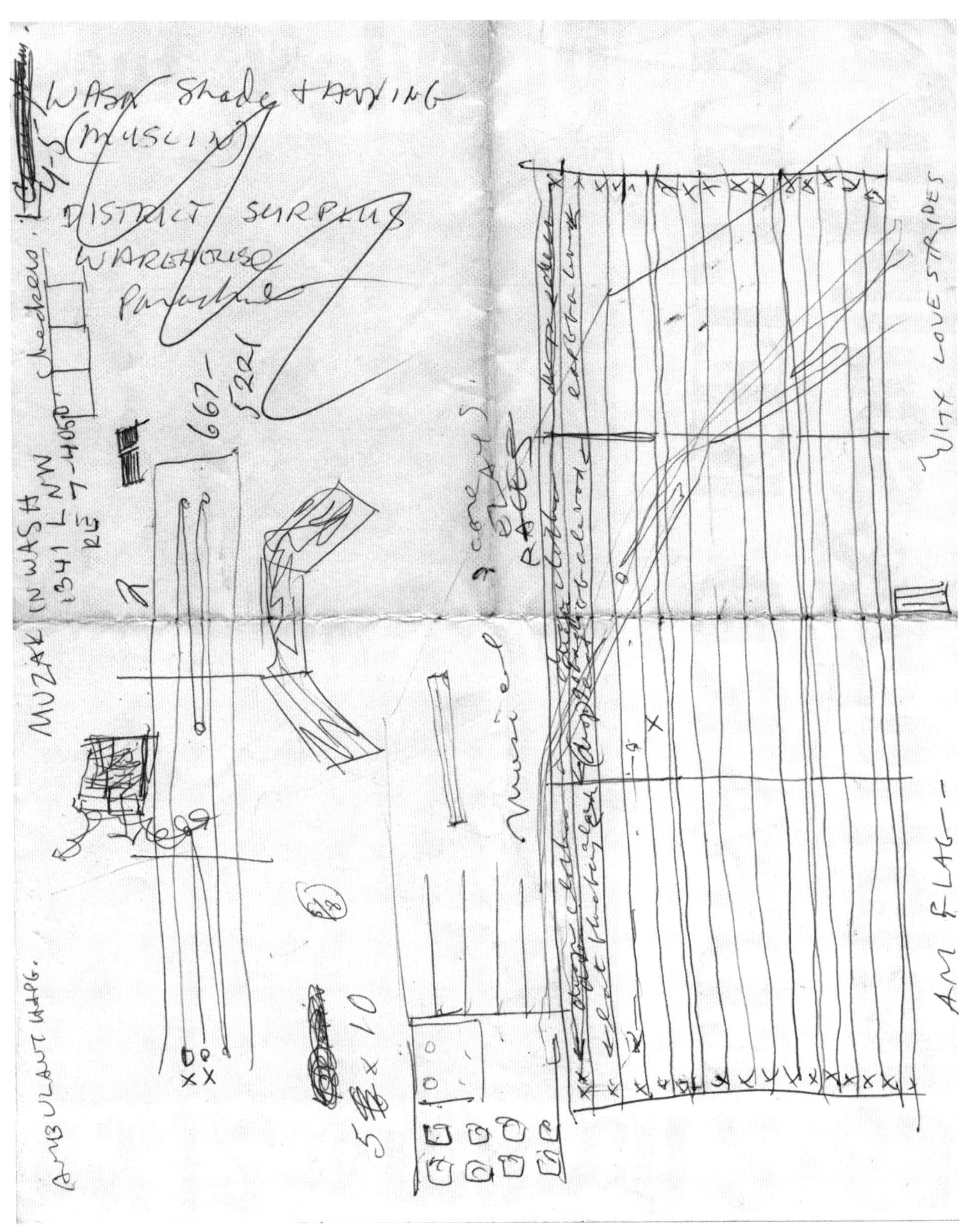

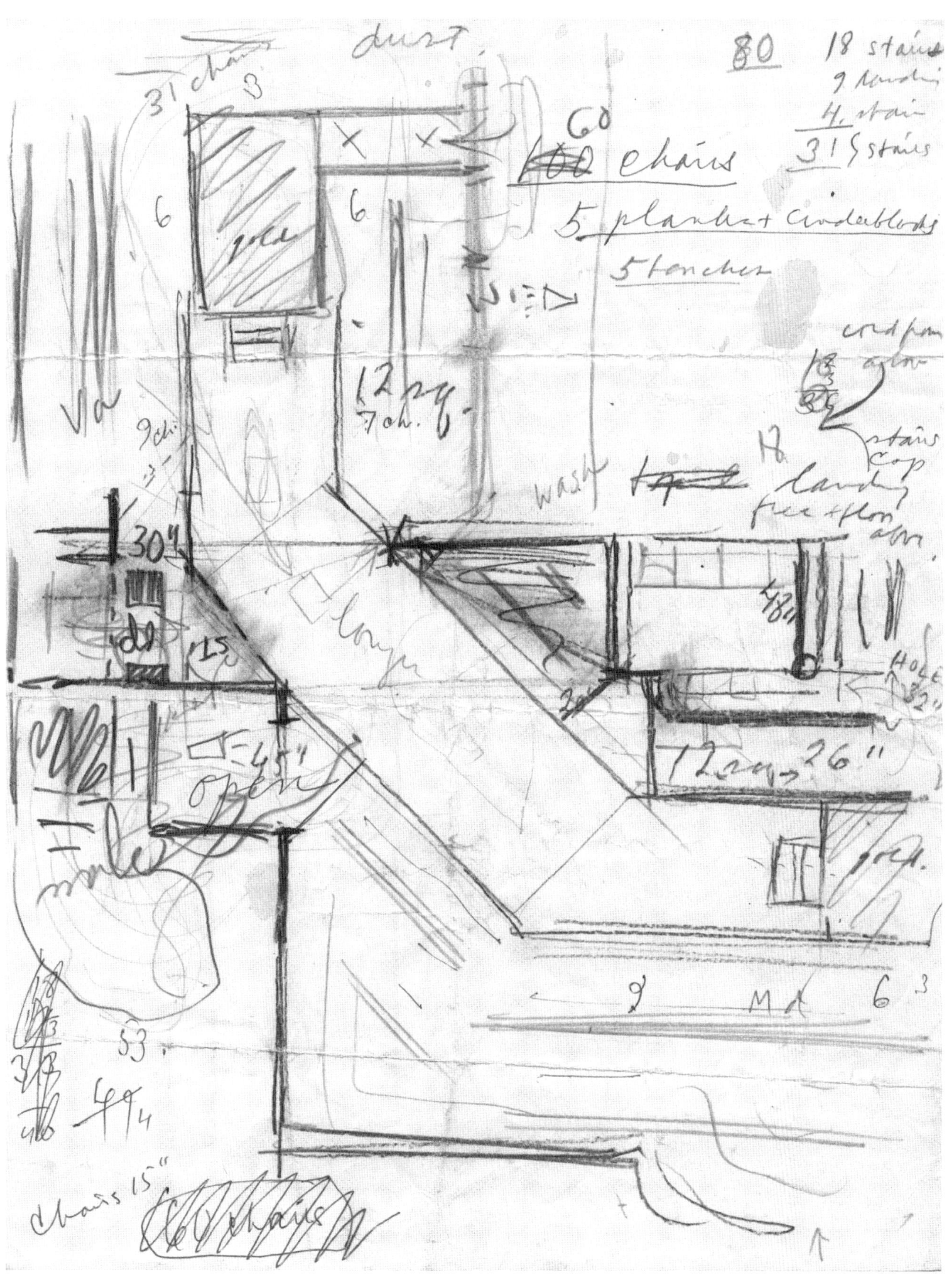

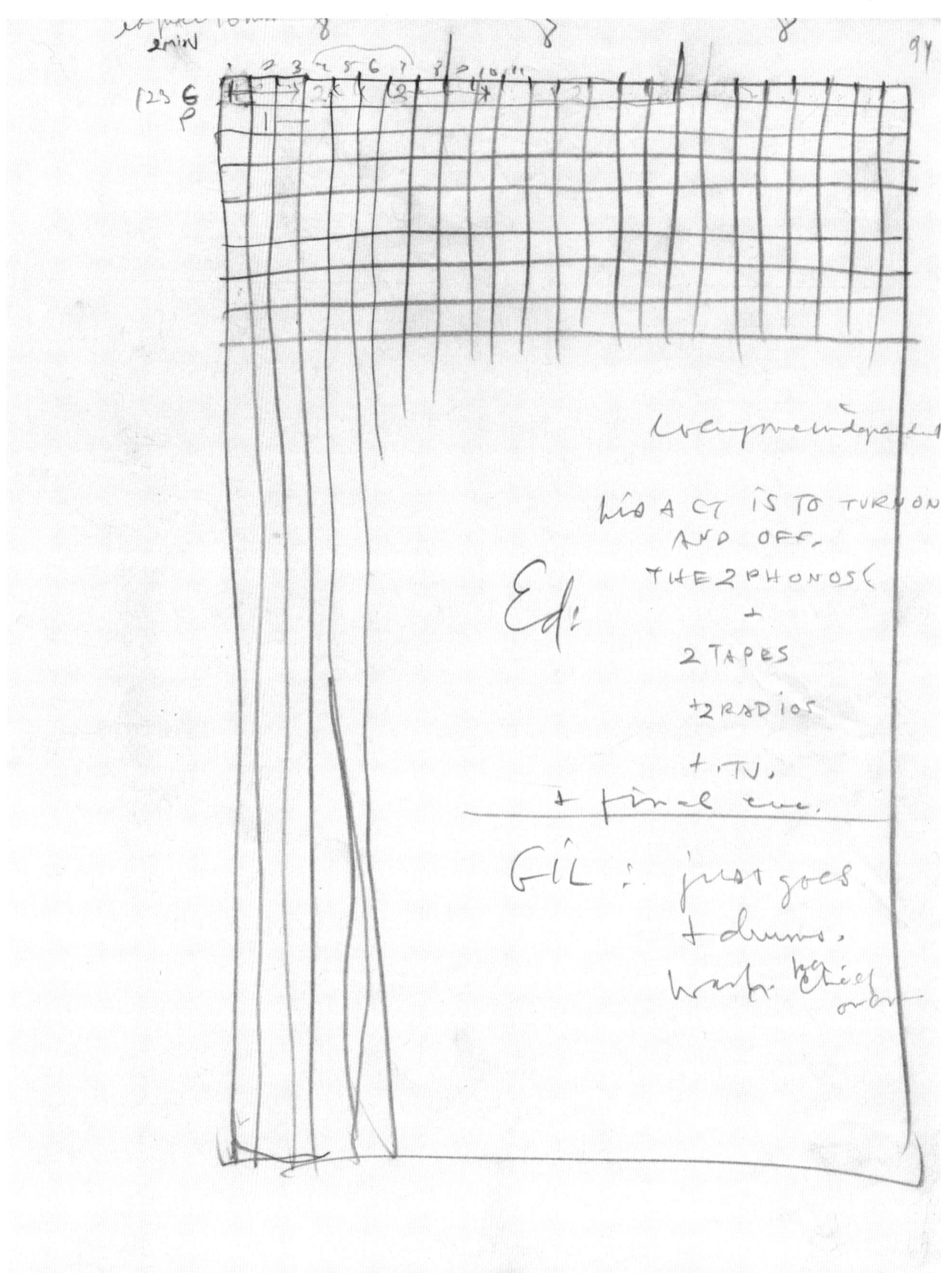
ED: A CT IS TO TURN ON
AND OFF.
THE 2 PHONOS (
+
2 TAPES
+2 RADIOS
+ TV,
+ final eve.
GIL : just goes
+ drums.

1965

soft
nolen

THE

MICKE·HOUSE

EXPANDED CINEMA +deflated
E   X   P   A   N   D $ Y
CINEMA
CINE by
Claes Oldenburg

CINE MATICK

1398 B

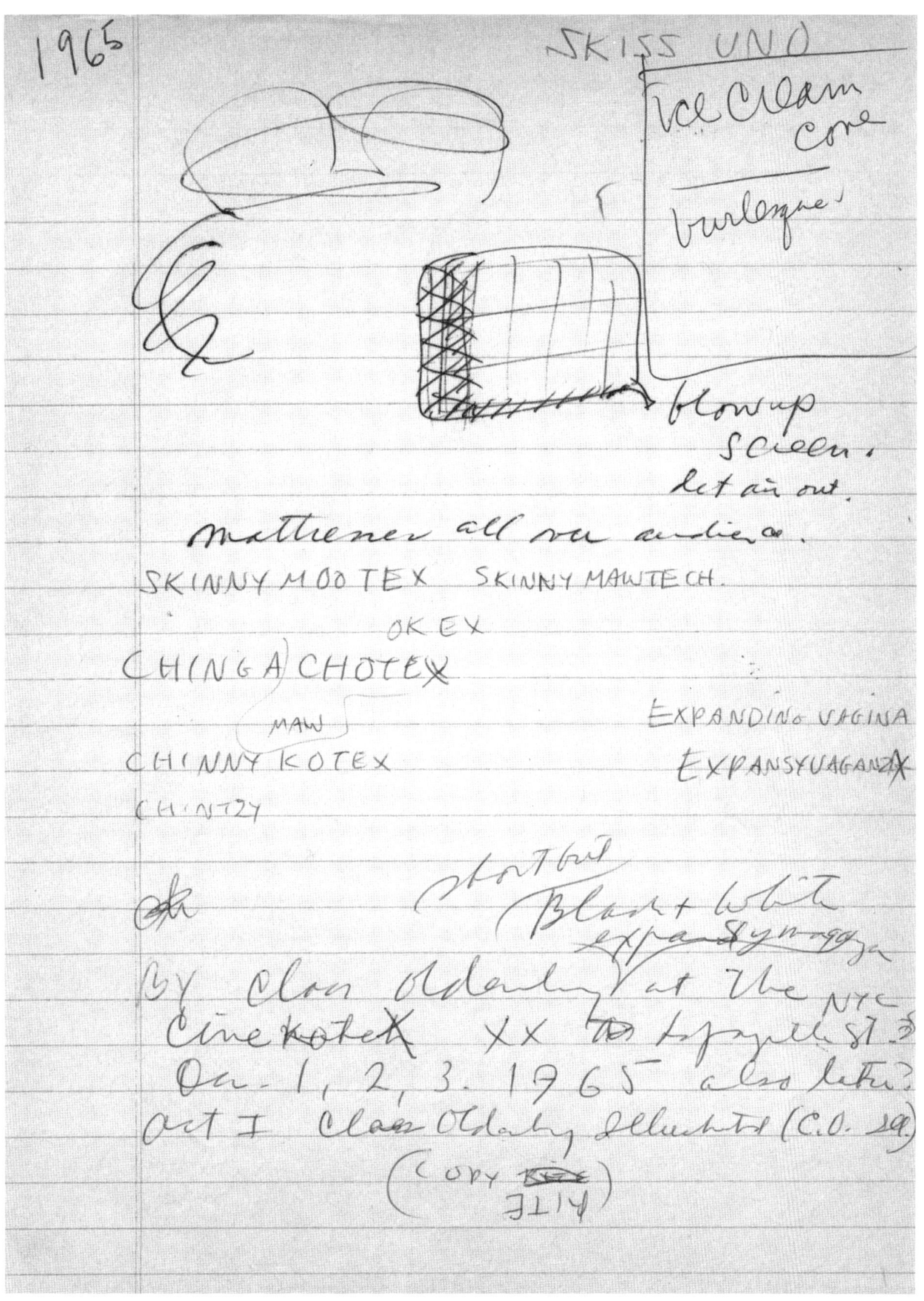

1965
SKISS UNO
Ice Cream
Cone
burlesque
blowup
screen.
let air out.
mattress all over audience.
SKINNY MOOTEX   SKINNY MAWTECH.
OK EX
CHINGA CHOTEX
MAW
EXPANDING VAGINA
CHINNY KOTEX
EXPANSYUAGANDA
CHINTZY
shortbut
Black + White
expandymoppa
By Claes Oldenburg at the
Cine Kotex   XX   Lafayette St.   NYC
Dec. 1, 2, 3, 1965   also later?
Act I   Claes Oldenburg Illustrates (C.O. 29)
(COPY
JITY)

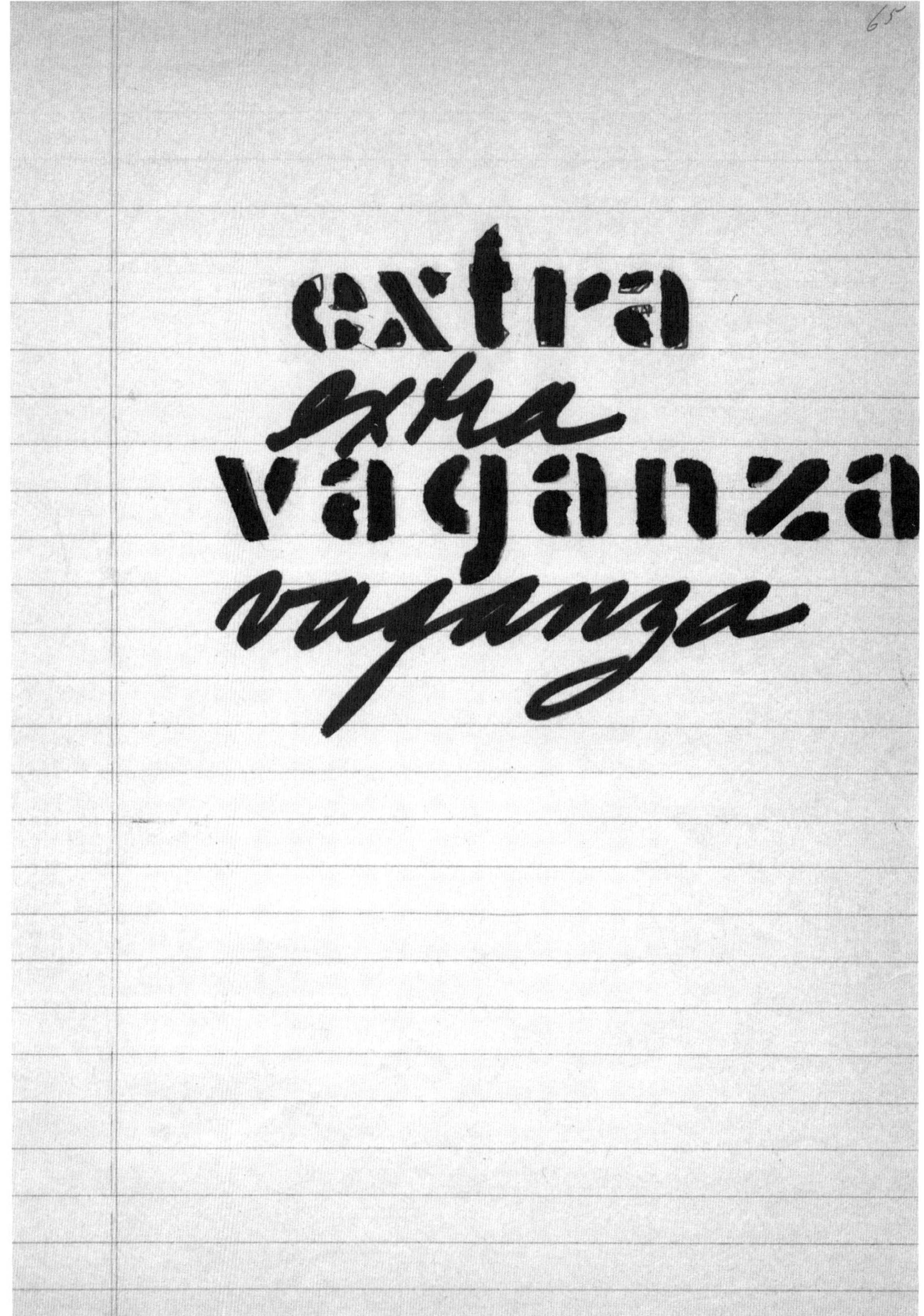

Sketch for an announcement

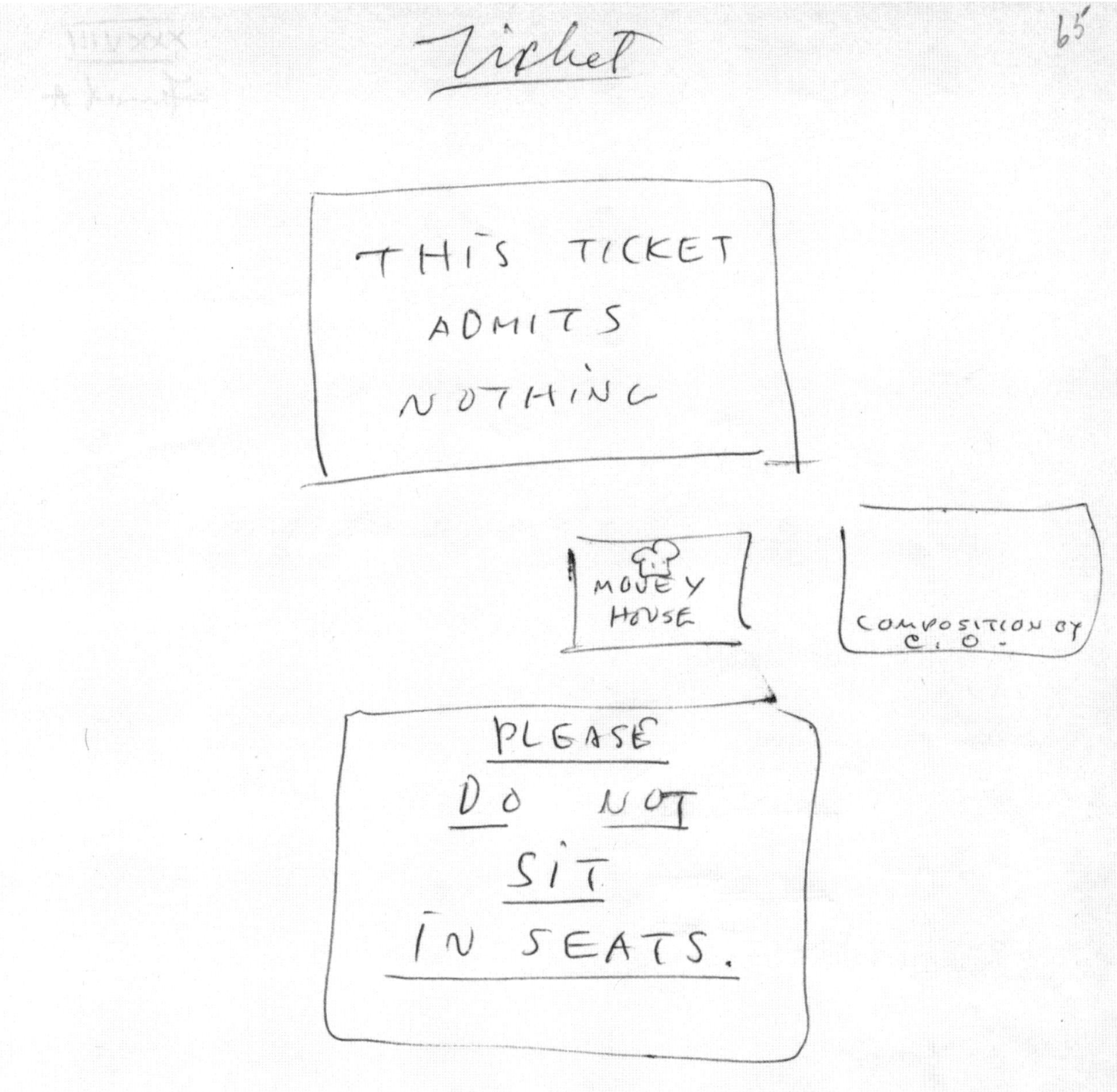

Sketch for a ticket

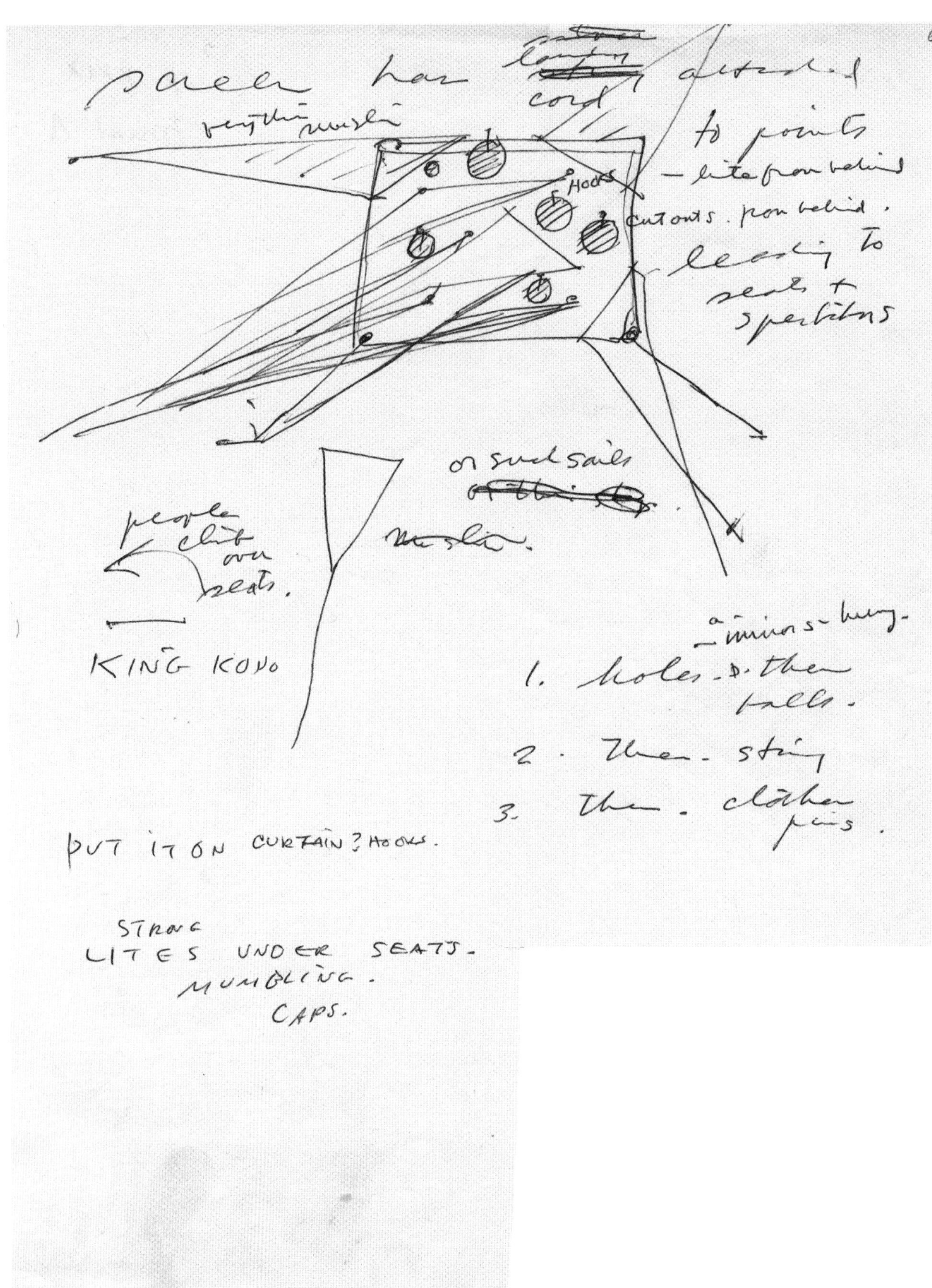
screen has lantern cord attached
very thin muslin
to points
— lite from behind
Hooks
cut outs . from behind .
leading to
seats +
spectators
or such sails
muslin .
people
climb
over
seats .
KING KONG
on such sails
a minors hung .
1. holes — & then
falls .
2. then — string
3. then — clothes
pins .
PUT IT ON CURTAIN ? HOOKS .
STRING
LITES UNDER SEATS .
MUMBLING .
CAPS .

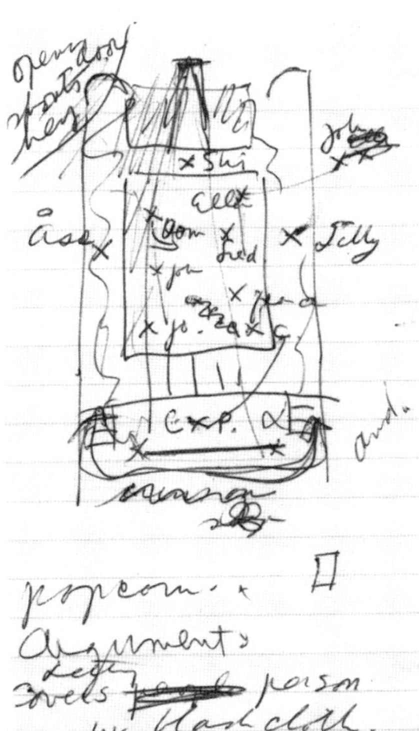

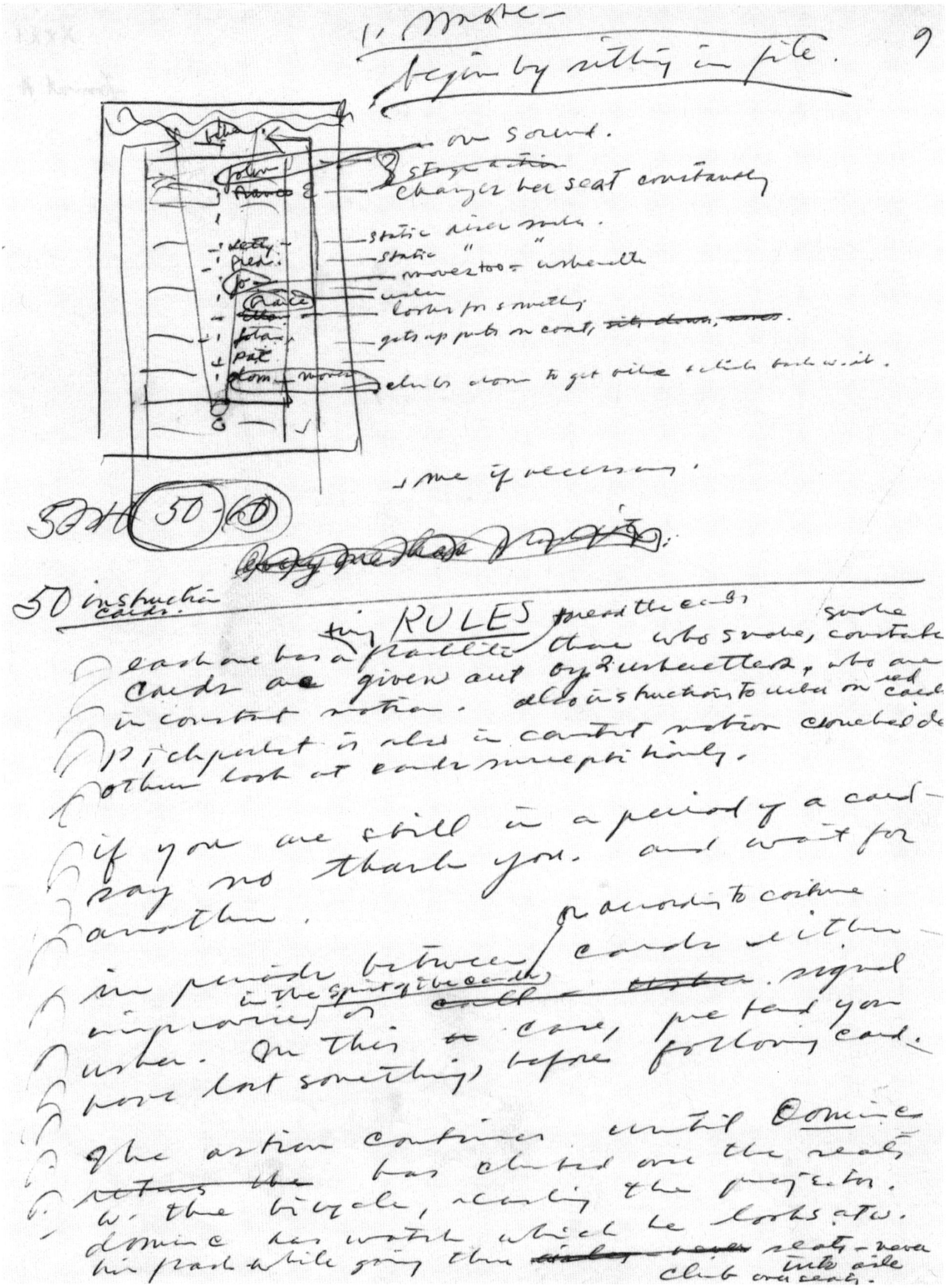

1. [illegible] —
Begin by sitting in pile.

on sound.

[illegible] stops action
changes her seat constantly

static river smoke.
static "   "
moves too — [illegible]
[illegible]
looks for something
gets up puts on coat, ~~sits down~~, ~~[illegible]~~

climbs down to get out [illegible] back w. it.

[illegible] me if necessary.

50 instruction
cards.

RULES

[much illegible handwritten text]

each one has a [illegible] to those who spoke, constant
cards are given out by 2 ushers, who are
in constant motion. also instructions to usher on card
pickpocket is also in constant motion crouched de
other look at each surreptitiously.

if you are still in a period of a card —
say no thank you. and wait for
another.

in periods between cards either
in the spirit of the cards ~~[illegible]~~. signal
usher. In this [illegible] case, pretend you
have lost something before following card.

the action continues until Domine
~~returns the~~ has climbed over the seats
w. the bicycle, nearing the projector.
Domine has watch which he looks at w.
his past while going through [illegible] seats — never
climb over seats.

Ticket size 10

```
┌─────────────────────────────┐
│                             │
│   STAND   UP                │   ← DO.
│   LOOK   AROUND             │
│                             │
│   ~~COUNT TEN~~             │   ← COUNT
│        10                   │
│                             │
└─────────────────────────────┘
```

~~Count~~ legit cards directly.
Any number may be included

count always at ~~same~~ set rate. If
~~action~~ ~~anda~~ counting ends before
action; sit down abruptly.

move one seat to right + left alternately
~~after~~ sitting down ~~from~~ after finishing a card
when reach edge find another seat = one row. male + female
Everyone has same bag of props — maybe groups.
    everyone has overcoat or some other garment. Exchanges.

collect tickets for next performance

fixed prep. — will or done without cards.
always count ten at least before ~~card~~ beginning
    action — wait longer if desired.

is better — whole pace should be slow
any variation or continuations allowed

little night music
for a movie
theatre.

Diner — steamy.

Trailer — 11

Beauty Shop — formal
(Antonioni)

Discotheque.

landscape → describe
disks
flaps.
lights.

seats.

mirror on head

juggling balls

apple

hats

can   cup   cup

tans.   glass. moon.

disk fat

(*) donuts.

fan pias

diagram of forms,
movie house

MASSAGE   *(DRIVE IN BATTLEFIELD)*
MASSACRE

Komposition för Moderna Museet

av

Claes Oldenburg

3*, 4, 6 och 7 oktober kl. 21.30 i museet

DJUR?

Med hjälp av

István Almay (Björn)   Pat Oldenburg (Sovande)
Gabrielle Björnstrand (Svamp)   Claes Oldenburg (Brevbärare)
Olle Granath (Massör)   Mette Prawitz (Sköterska)
Six Maix (Björn)   Rico Weber (Björn)

och
några andra
som hjälper till med att lägga sig

och
åskådare som också lägger sig
så småningom

Föreställningen varar ungefär 45 min.

* generalrepetition

Plate XXXV corresponds to 115:6–115:23 in text

TIME

positioning tape.

the tape sound of the typewriter.

it then says please lie down (for a long time.) FILM SLOW. MON AM.

[other tape? at same time]

From time to time draw back curtain and growls. from wardobe 2 TIMES?

(difficult section)

Pat turns in her sleep   perhaps a baloon breaks (a fart)

BAMBOO POLE   BEARS   NURSES

Gabrielle draws on b board. at bedroom wall — LIGHTING (OLD PROJ. - SLIDE VIEWER)

Other film goes on. or what action

When people are down

X. Sleep Trip dreams

? Hawaiian song   King serenade at 33.   [dreams]

Bears emerge w. turlp tops of leaves + "riis"

Ga brielle walks about ... RED SAIL RISES

Pat wakes up. some pops then more then more

+ gabrielle.   X

Says 'wake up' — WIDOR again   after lunch

Front door now opens up coat room opens lights go on. We start

clean up put sculptures back etc.

As people leave Varm Korv outside.

take red out of Tube. roll up tube at bedroom wall.

Olle? MASSAGE TUBE or ? work w. Olle, me demonstrate.

(Someone to watch tapes + lites.)

FORMS of MASSAGE.   SKY STUFF

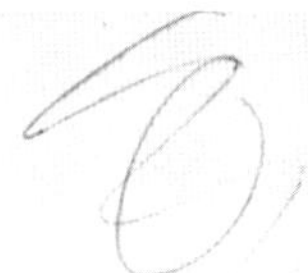

MASSAGE

I. <u>Approach and Diversion in Sculpture Garden</u> etc.

The spectators coming to the Museum climb the hill towards the Museum
finding the Museum lights out. It is completely dark inside and there
is a sign on the door: STÄNGT.
The floodlight illuminating the right side of the building is ~~on~~ casting
shadows of the spectators as they are guided around the right side of the
building, past the garden, through the outdoor cafe and into the Museum
by a side door, where they buy tickets and wait. *waving a sculpt. on rope.*
~~(And take off their coats.)~~
As they pass the Sculpture Garden (Picasso sculptures in concrete) they
see a Biological Museum Tableau: Two Bears who come to life from time to
time and lift (seemingly) the sculptures out of the ground and break them
up. (The "Picasso" which is lifted is made of grey cardboard, drawn on.
Thus the sculptures are returned to the original cardboard material)

Time:

Lights: — *spot in front*

Sound: — *none .*

-2-

MASSAGE

II. <u>Disrobing (Av**k**lädning)</u>   (and <u>Waiting for the Performance to Begin</u>)

The coats of the spectators are taken by two women wearing hygienic
masks (like nurses). Passed by them to three helpers who take the
coats (as if stealing them and with the suggestion of uncertainty as
to their destination), carry them into the wardrobe. The wardrobe is
located in the main room some distance away.
In the wardrobe the helpers hang the coats on "floating" hooks (they
are so constructed, sets of 40 or so on grids attached to ceiling) to
make a full effect (there will not be enough coats to fill the space).
Like a forest or an organ or a huge choir. Or like hanging coats.
(give no checks first night and see if confusion results)

Time:

Lights:

Sound:

MASSAGE   -3-

II 413 <u>Tableaux:</u> (Mass) <u>Walk to Wardrobe.</u>

The spectators are admitted to the main room from the entrance
at the opposite end of the long room. Up to this time this door
has been shut.   (They have been handing over their wraps through
the counter at the door into the Museum collection room)
They are guided to the Wardrobe past the Exhibits by Mette who
wheels a TELE orange bicycle, straddling it from time to time or
turning it upside down. She wears a red costume (athlete top and
boxer trunks and white stockings?) and hygienic mask. She says
repeatedly: "My mother told me never to play with food."
Reaching the Wardrobe which is covered by a curtain, she puts down
the bike (stands it upside down?). Pulls the curtain aside as if
revealing a monument, revealing the "stolen" coats hung. This scene
is brightly illuminated in pink and blue and yellow lights.
(Music: Widor organ Toccata has been playing since beginning of III.)
(Is there a sign reading: Though the objects invite touch, we ask you
not to... the swedish sign at my exhibit)
Mette remains here showing the Wardrobe until after the Toccata ends
and through the following passage of Lion Roars. At the end of the
Lion Roars she closes curtain again.
(She opens the curtain 3 minutes about later when the roars return,
and so on. The roars return at 3 minute intervals through the sound
of the Typewriter (which begins after the end of the first set of
roars).

                                                      contd

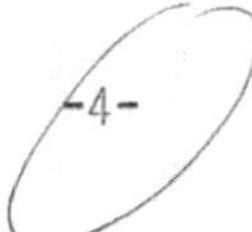

-4-

MASSAGE

Mette is on the main floor when the Lion Roars are not on, helping with
the Gymnastics (Blankets and Warm Mory) and Tucking People In and then
helping them to Wake. (Without her bicycle).

The Exhibits which the spectators pass on their way to the Wardrobe are
the following:

1) 200 folded Army blankets (with newspapers) and a warm sausage on them
   (like cemetery) neatly placed in rows (like knäckebröd).

2) Olle, in white rubber overalls with (how) a giant 400 cm long toothpaste tube hung from the ceiling rafters.

3) Two "Bears" in an enclosure eating knäckebröd and wrapping one another
   in newspapers with twine.

4) Gabrielle, in front of the light from an old slide projector (in which
   are stencils of letters?) at a blackboard, drawing lines with chalk
   and the aid of a white ruler. On the lines she writes SKJUT and DRAG
   over and over. She wears a hygienic mask, a blue nurses costume with
   haddress. To her forearms are attached long bamboo poles which reach
   to an attachment on the rafters of the ceiling (?).

5) Claes running up and down the stairs to the "Hyllan" in gym shoes
   tracing his path with bright orange string back and forth back and
   forth (too tiring?).

6) Pat as Pytt i Panna in a brown pajamas to which "white boiled potatoes"
   are attached, one a bed of pillows of thin muslin stuffed with blown
   up blue baloons, covered with a giant fried egg.

Time: Widor 16 min. max. Lion about 4 min.   Total: 20 min.

Lights: Small light over Pat, Projector at Gabrielle

Sound: Widor Toccata and Lion Roars

XL

-5-

MASSAGE

IV. Gymnastics

Cue to the beginning of this section is the beginning of the sound of
the typewriter (at 1 7/8). Cue for the beginning of the typewriter
is the end of the Lion Growls in the Wardrobe.
Claes (or another operator) turns on the Typwriter tape on Machine no. 2.
which is located in the main hall against inside wall.
Simultaneously a projection begins of a film in which Claes demonstrates
the use of the blanket and warm sausage and newspaper found for the use
of the audience at this time.
The audience is drawn by the film showing away from the Wardrobe which
is closing and should occupy an area in the center about of the main
hall.

Mette instructs as well how to use the blankets etc.

Meanwhile the action of the others at their stations (continues as described) and with additions (plot). Pat turns in her sleep popping a baloon
or two.

Time: About 15 min. of typewriter. At 3 min. periods, 3 min. of Lion
       Growls

Lights:

Sound: Tape of Typewriter.

        Tape of Lion Growls

        (A supplementing tape machine may bed out of synch with the others
         to enrich the sound.)

-6-

MASSAGE

~~VI. Rest (VII)~~

The ~~instruction~~ film ends by me wrapping the ~~blanket around me and lying down.~~ ~~(On Mon. I will do the instructions in person)~~

The people are helped to do so until as many as possible are bedded down. ~~When the typewriter tape ends, the Hawaiian tape begins. This is the cue for people to be helped to lie down.~~

The audience is supplied with blindfolds (?)

While the spectators are blindfolded and tucked in and ~~the Hawaiian music plays~~ the Bears emerge eating knäckebröd, carrying "ris" such as used by streetcleaners and carrying burlap bags of autumn leaves (stenciled LÖV), which they place about.

Mette says: ~~Sleep now.~~

~~Olle raises the giant tube and draws from it long red tube (?)~~

~~At this time if the spectators are lying, another film may be shown perpendicular to the instruction film the length of the main hall on the back of the Bedroom Room wall.~~

Time: Hawaiian music 13 min.

Lights:

Sound: Hawaiian Music.

MASSAGE

VI.   (End)

Widor Toccata after Hawaiian Music.

Mette says "Wake Up!" Opens the Wardrobe closet.

The Front Doors opened by the Bears. A bright light shines in. The
Bears go outside to raise a flag dipped in plaster.

We pick up, leaves, bits of sausage etc.

Put sculptures back

Time:

Lights: Outside a bright light

Sound: Widor Toccata indefintely

STRUCTURES

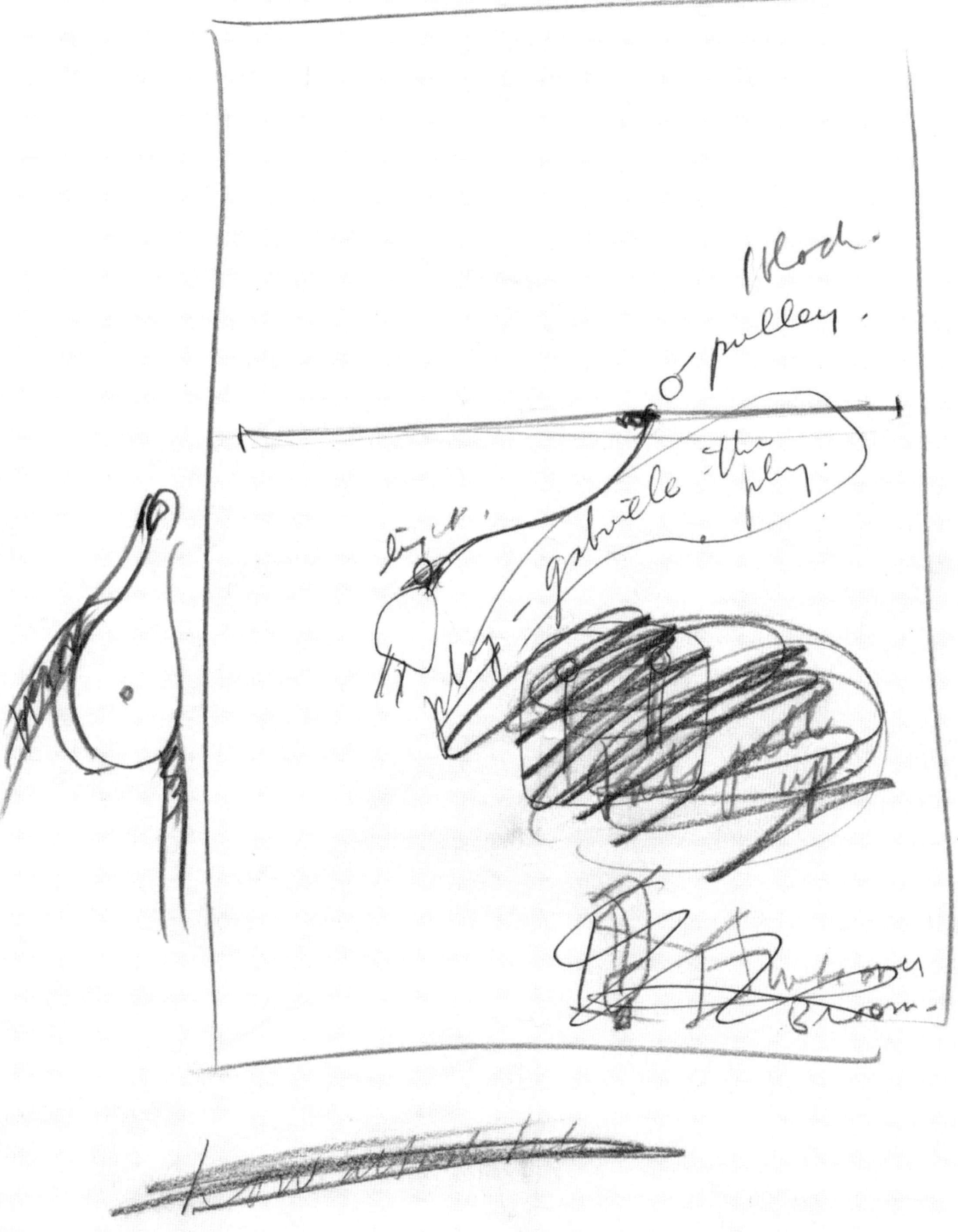

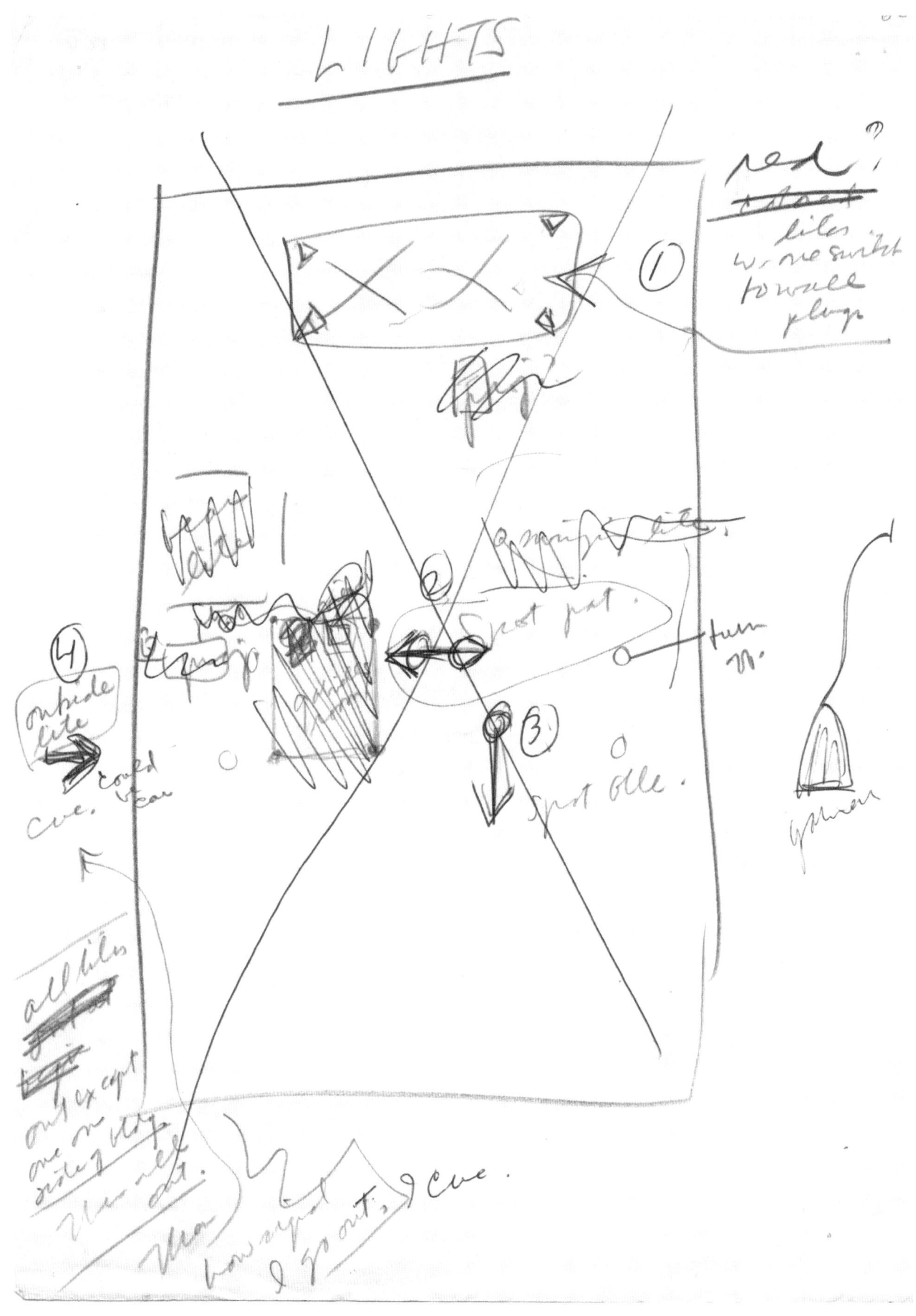

LIGHTS
red ?
①
②
③
④
outside lite
spot pat.
spot olle.
all tiles

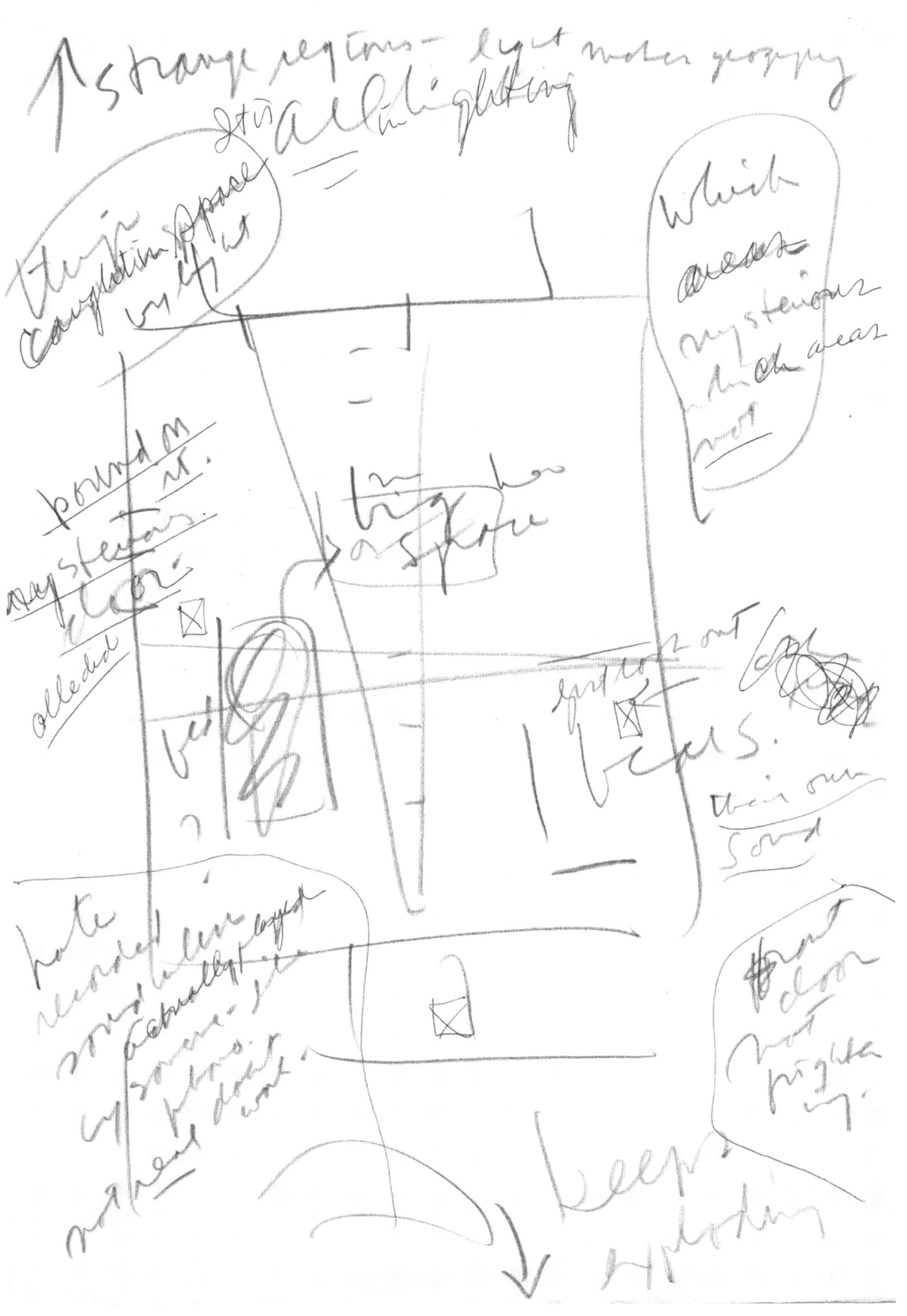

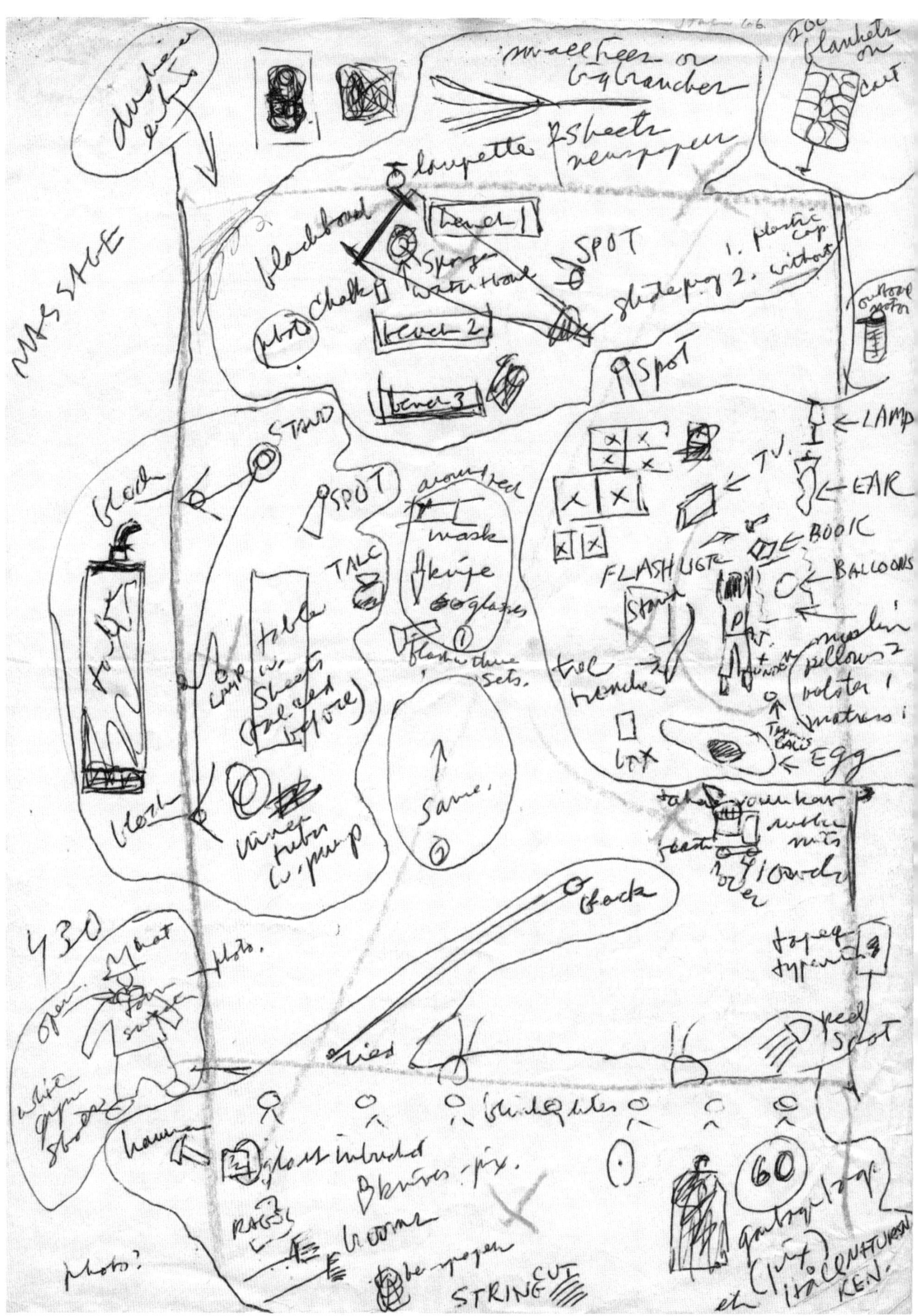

Stage plan showing location of objects used in the performance

THEORY AND PREPARATION

12/25

DRAW
(MORE)
CLIP

---

1. THEORY – WRITTEN

Early thoughts: the pattern of rectangles.

Page or two of notes, typed, spoken &
drawn and clipped.

---

1. *DRAWING* SECRETARIES,
~~Sewing~~ of boss's costume – others'. /
DRAWING
~~Building~~ of the boss's soft office.
DRAWING
~~Sewing~~ of a giant pencil and typewr. eraser.

---

1. *(PHOTO AND)*
~~KRATTANECIA QLECTURES~~ *ACCOUNT*
I work up the boss's activities in my
office. [at studio + on sites]
(PHOTO AND
ACCOUNT)
I visit a stationery store.
ACCOUNT +
I study a watercooler, filming it. ~~DEA~~

I study a desktop full of office equipment.
ACCOUNT
(AND PHOTO)
I select players. *?*
ACCOUNT

3.

~~Entrance of audience~~ *+ TYING UP*

A dirty secretary

~~Secretary costumes~~

3.

(I direct.)

Leg behavior. *OFFICE BODY/BEHAVIOR*

Contents of a drwer shown

How to wash floor and desk, pursuing spectators into chairs.

Installation of tape recorders on thighs. *OR RADIOS*

Birth of a phone.

3.

Typewriter behavior

How to bend over *(FILE)*

~~Tying up of audience~~

Use of desk lamp

~~What to say~~ *ACCOUNT*

Disposal of boss *ATTACK ON ME SMASHING OF OFFICE*

SCENARIO

12/25

WRITE

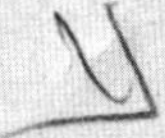

3.   TYPOGRAPHICAL

Sounds and words (to be said and recorded)
in column beside the scenario proper. →

?

WHAT TO SAY (ACCOUNT)   TRANSCRIPTS.

SOUNDS DESCRIBED

PAGE
NATURE OF A MEDIUM — SOUND MUST BE
IMAGINED.

~~INCIDENTS~~

12/25

ACT
IN
PHOTO
STUDIO

THE USE OF PHOTOS:

3.

Comparison of drawn or clipped proposal
with actual execution. ~~list of photos~~
Before After   Fantasy/reality
Event/sublimation of event
~~photo 1~~   ~~photo 2~~ PHOTO

Also: Actual event - fantasy - sublimation
~~photo 1~~   ~~photo 2~~   ~~photo 3~~
PHOTO   CLIPS   PHOTO.
                ETC.

PHOTO = REAL

3.   photo 1   photo 2
Also: what I see   - what other sees
       what I imgine- what other imagines

       The period (of preparation with
       others in which
       I receive the material of others
       events are created by others
       My prepared material is cross-bred
       with that of others

Appeal of the photo is thats its both real and fantasy
Like vision the photo is both real and unreal, but it is real.
Which scenario to print, the unreal or real or both?

12
26

THEORY AND PREPARATION 12/25

1.

ACCOUNT.

Studying office behavior. Coffee lady.

LIMITS OF THE MEDIUM (PAGES) AND TIME:

CONSTRUCTION AND
OBTAINING OF PROPS
ELIMINATED.

SUGGESTIONS AND
ACCOUNTS ONLY

NO PHOTOS EXC. CLIPS

2

GRAND VIEW OF FINALE

ACT
ON SITE
DRAW

4.

~~Deafening sounds described~~ PHOTO ON
SITE
~~Boss smashing office~~
All asleep ~~etc.~~ on desks

Big Screens with images STRIP IN

~~Add: Interpretation~~

add:
Expense List.

6

Set *Site*

Props   Costumes   ~~help to make them~~
draw

Cast

audience in
Can fake hidden ~~and~~ big view .

machinery
Sound will not be necessary *for paper presentation.*

Editor and Layout
who.

a. SELECT
b. INTERPRET

what specialist

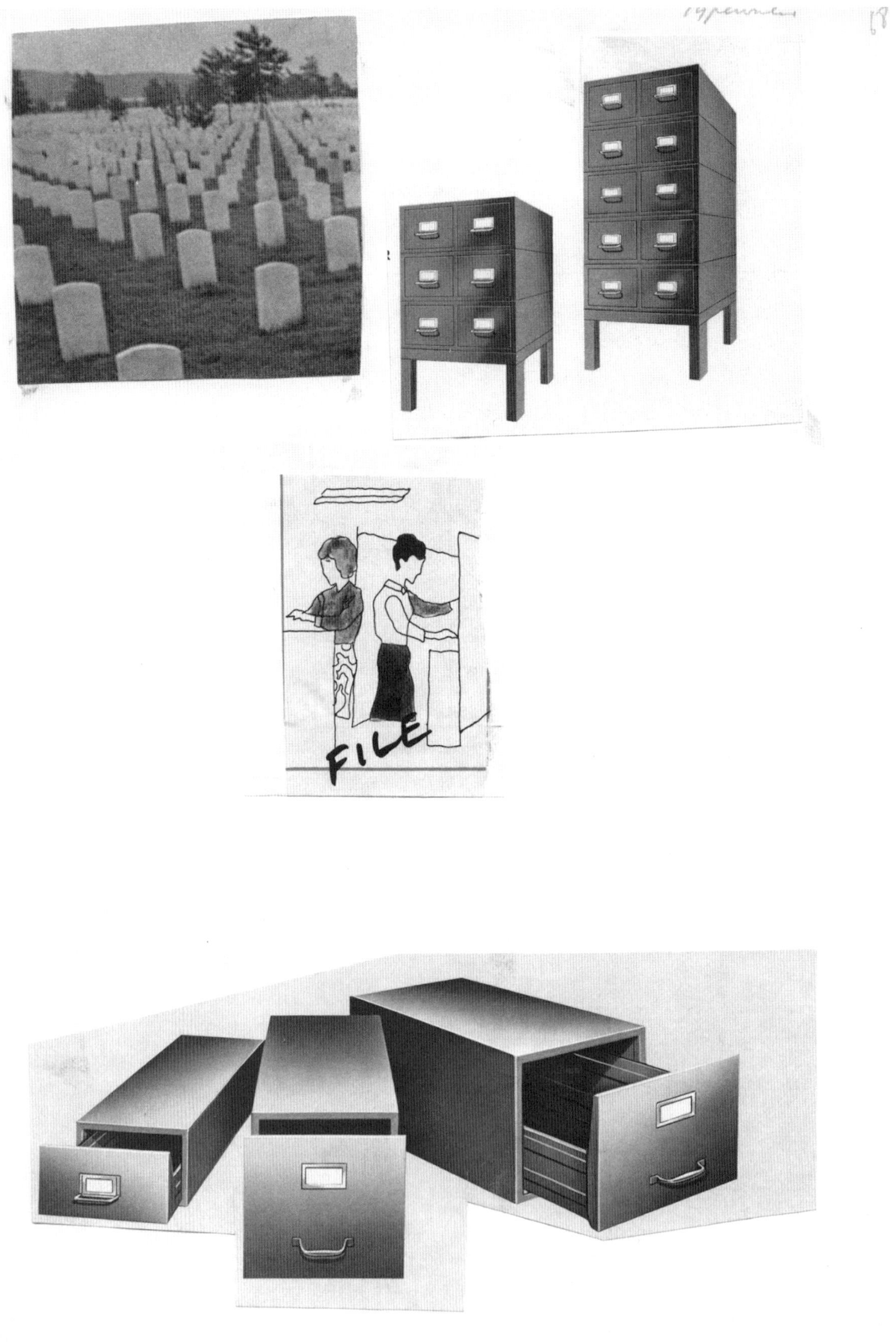

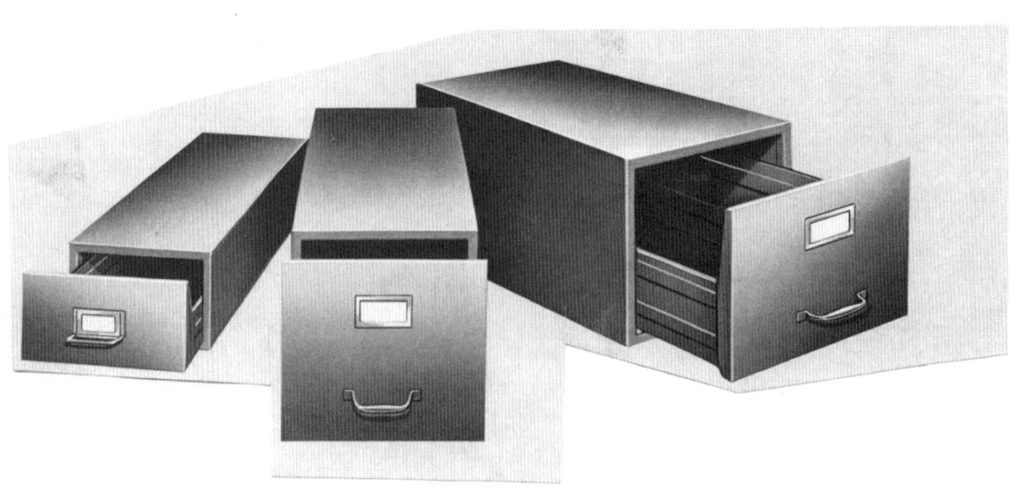

Clippings

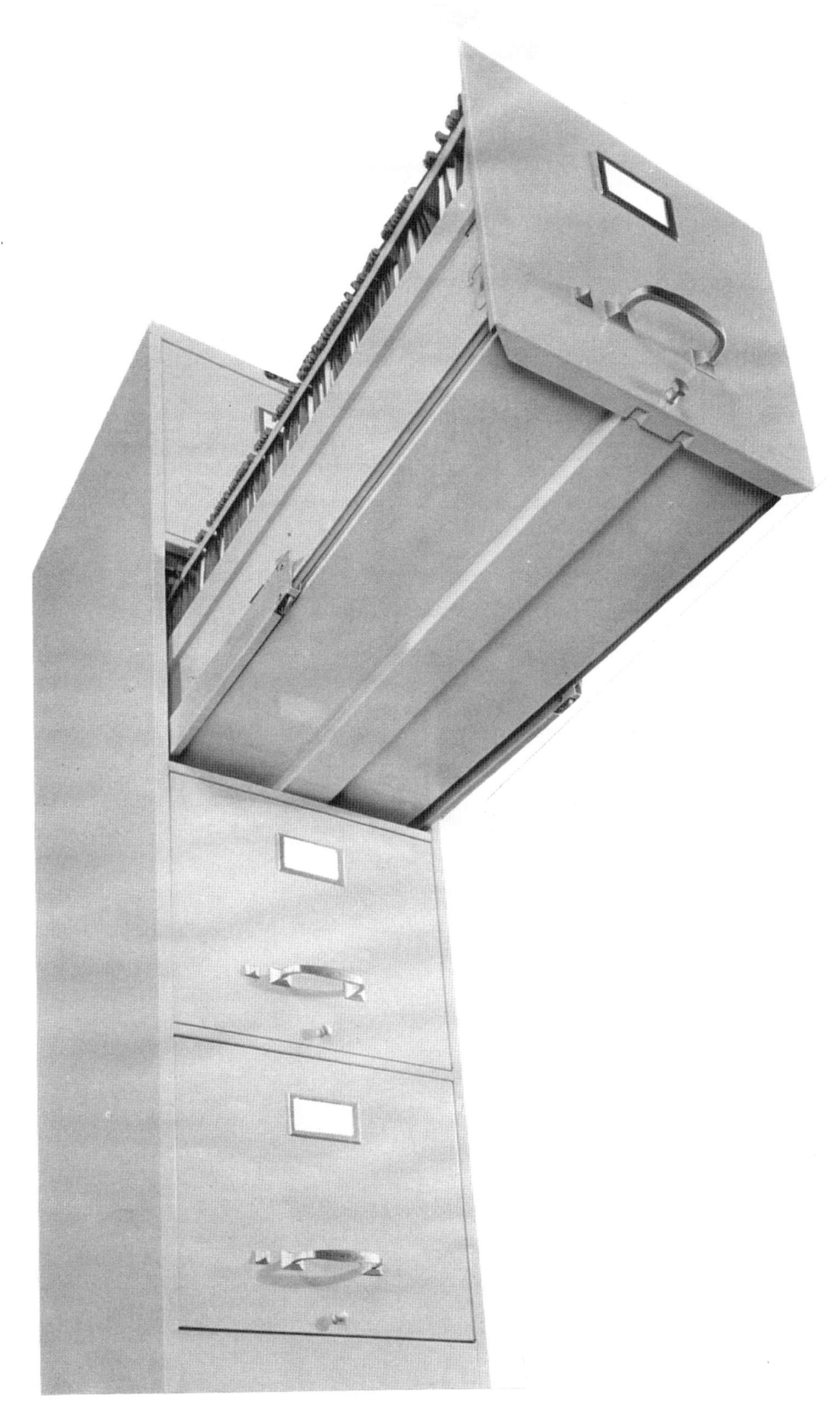

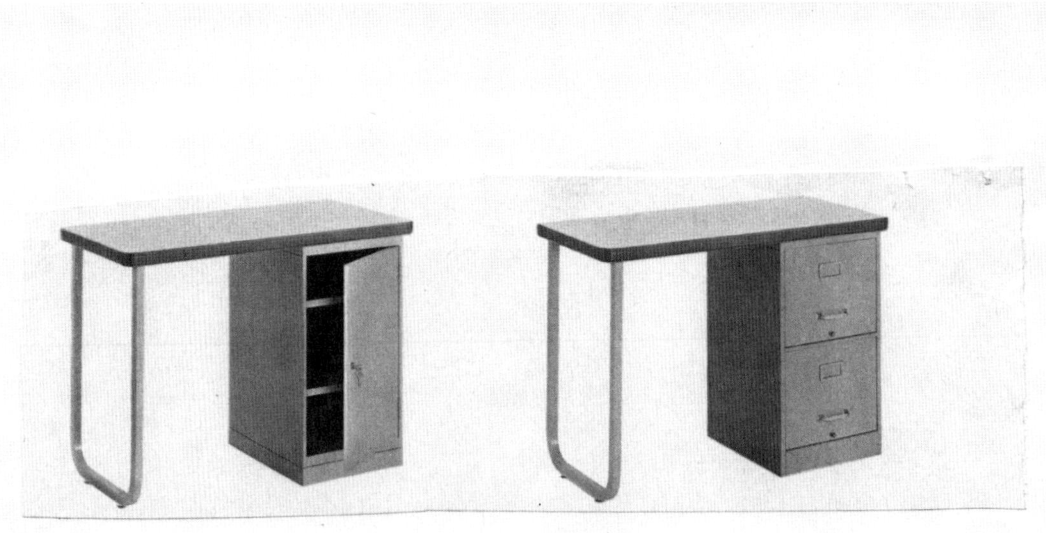

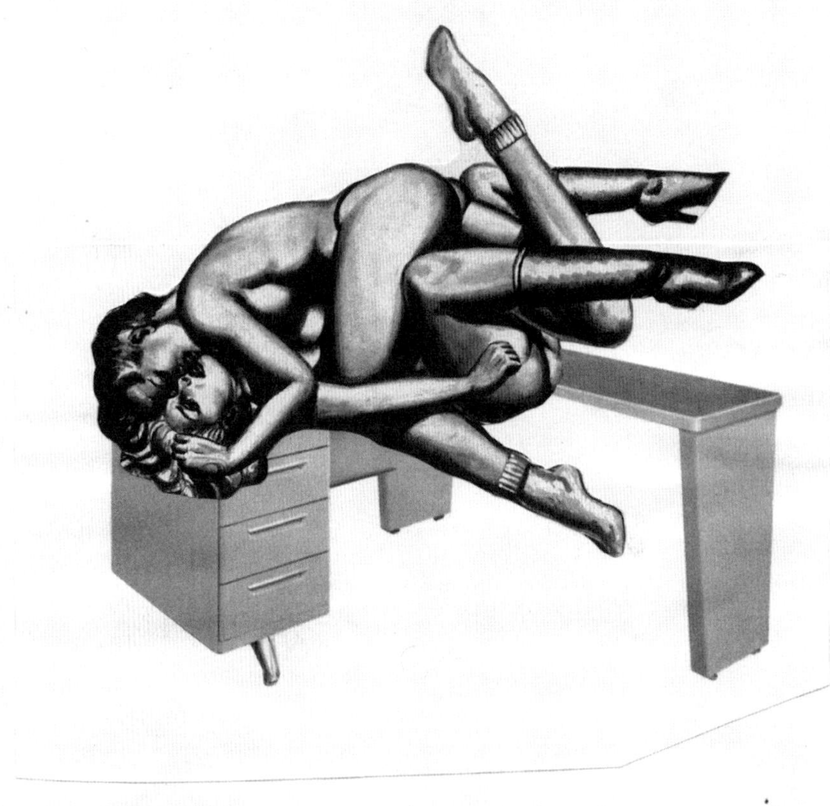

LIX

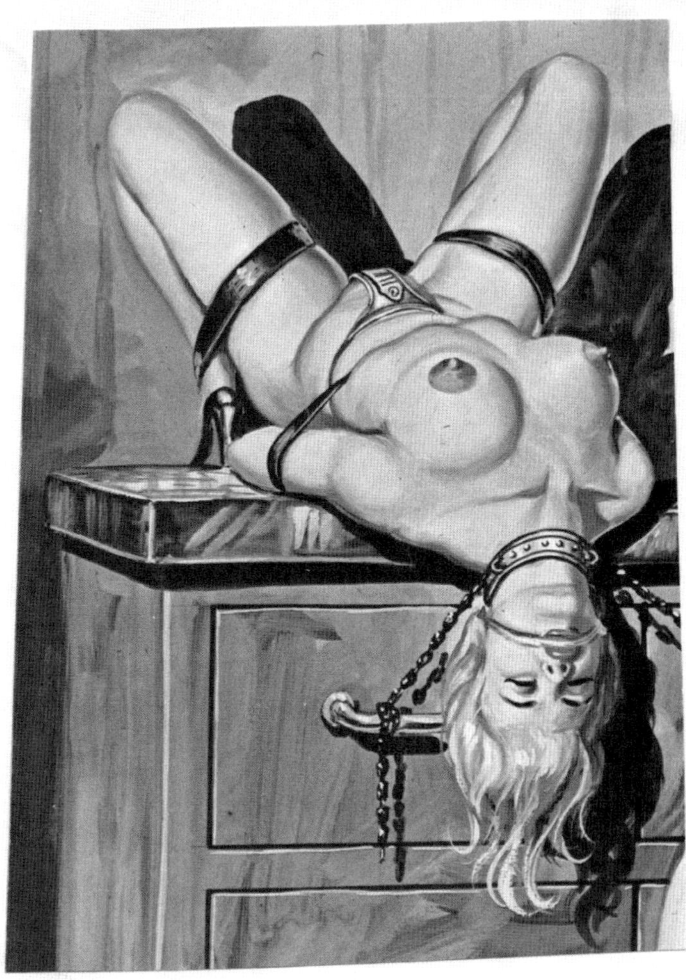

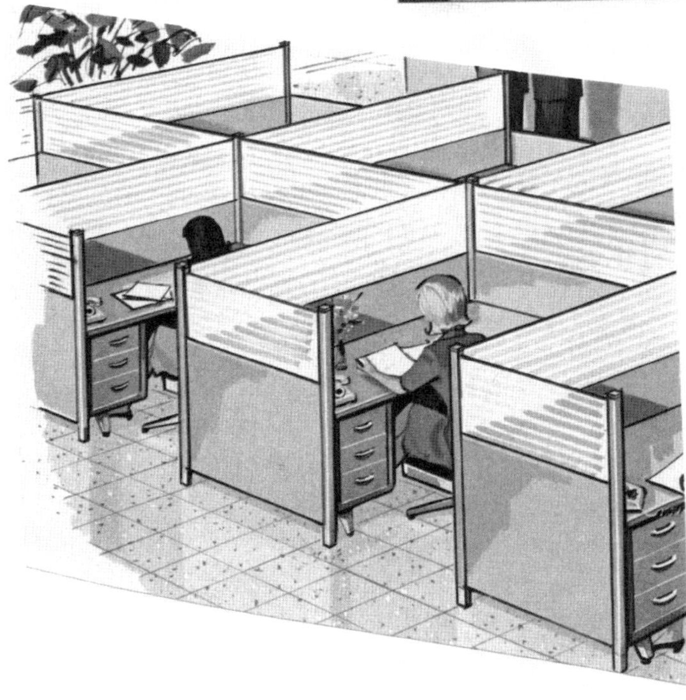

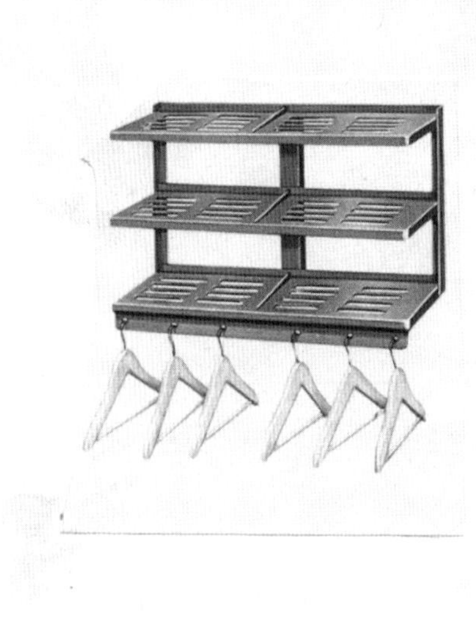

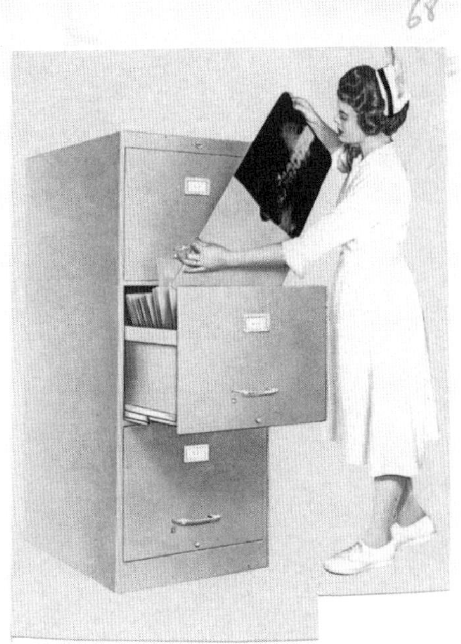

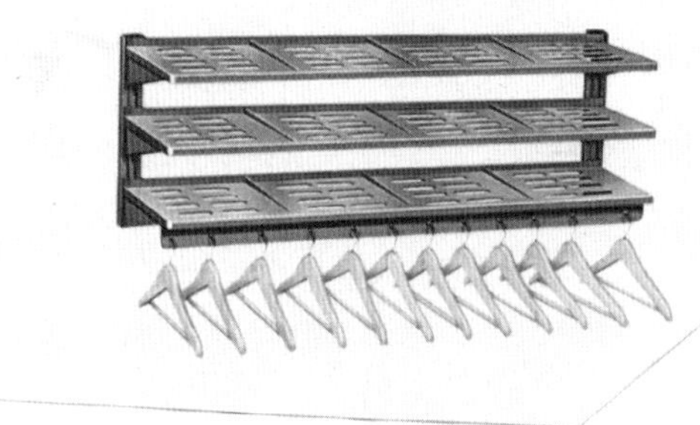

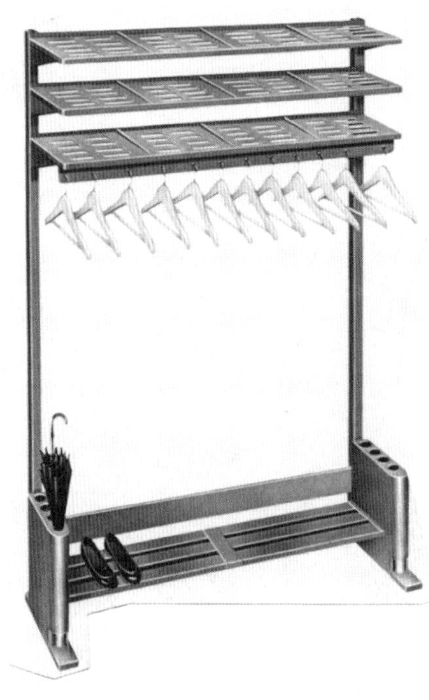

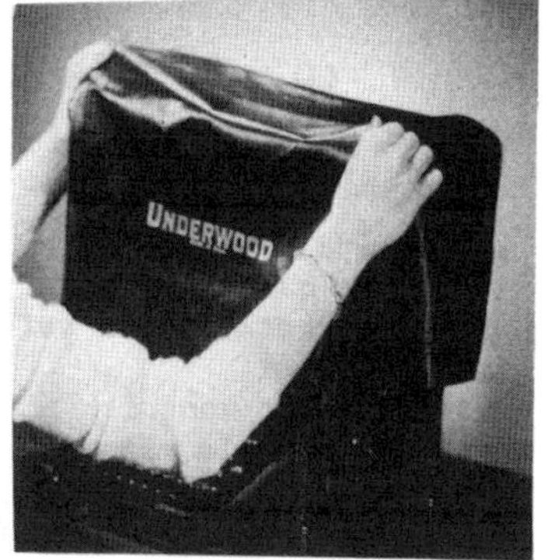
UNDERWOOD

grey 2
size 3

grey 1
size 2

white
size 1

Typing

Typing

Buzzing
Ringing
Dialing
Adding
Bookkeeping
Sharpening
Ticking
 Duplicating
Stapling

MACHINE

Sneezing   Slapping
Breathing   Blowing
XXXXXXXXX   Belching
Farting   Whistling
Coughing   Humming
Yawning   Scratching
Chewing
Groaning
Laughing

BODY

Stamping   Tapping
Slamming   Cutting
Crumpling   Ripping
Walking   Clicking
Squeaking   Flipping
Opening   Clinking
Closing   *Banging*
kicking   *Turning*
Jingling

OBJECT-AGENT

in add. to these maybe some words, from a secretarial
manual. And overhear more office noises

graph paper.

g

W. note

Preparatory study for illustration

Plates LXIV–LXVI:
Illustration as it appeared in
"Esquire" Magazine, May 1969

Stamping Squeaking Ringing
x Typing Coughing Buzzing Hu
g Squeaking Clicking Addin
g Ringing Slamming Tapping
Chewing Walking Sharpeni
ing Typing Typing Clicking Sla
Sneezing Breathing Coughing W
Breathing Farting Yawni
ng Walking Humming Slamming
oughing Clicking Adding Typing Clic
ialing Sneezing Groaning Dialingt
Ticking Adding Ringing Tapping
lamming Typing Slamming
g Sharpening Dialing Banging Adding
pping Yawning Ringing Crumpling
aking Slamming Buzzing
Typing Belching Chewing Tappi
g Adding Humming Sharpening Yawni
aling Squeaking Buzzing Clicking
amming Typing AddingBuzzing Sne
Walking Coughing Squeaking Dialli
Breathing Clicking Scratching Chew
ng Walking Yawning Tapping Crumpli
ing Banging Dialing Humming Crump
g Tapping Adding Coughing Clicking
ingChewing Stamping Slamming O
Stamping Banging Closing Sharpening
eaking Typing Groaning Crumpling
ing Yawning Coughing Tapping Ripping
Buzzing Coughing Tapping Bang
ing Chewing Farting Stampi
g Walking Ringing Coughing Slammi
Typing Clicking Sneezing Blowi
ing Coughing Groaning
ng Stamping Sharpening Yawning
gCrumpling Adding Sneezi

Walking Groaning Walking
Dialing
Sneezing Adding Yawning Cli
Groaning Typing Walking Ty
Stamping Squeaking Ringing Ticki
Coughing Buzzing Humming
Slamming Clicking Adding T
Typing Walking Tapping Sharpening Typi
Typing Clicking Slamming
Breathing Coughing Walki
Farting Yawning
Walking Humming Slamming Clicki
Clicking Adding Typing Clicking Add
Sneezing Groaning Dialing Stampi
Adding Ringing Tapping B
Typing Slamming Typi
Sharpening Dialing Banging Adding Wa
Yawning Ringing Crumpling Humm
Slamming Buzzing
Belching Chewing Tapping Co
Humming Sharpening Yawning
Squeaking Buzzing Clicking St
Typing Adding Buzzing Sneezin
Coughing Squeaking Walking Dialing
Clicking Scratching Chewing Slamm
Walking Yawning Tapping Crumpling Di
Banging Dialing Humming Crumpling
Adding Coughing Clicking Walki
Stamping Slamming Openin
Banging Closing Crump
Typing Groaning Crumpling Sharpening Rip
Coughing Groaning Tapping Ripping Banging
Chewing Farting Stamping Buzz
Walking Ringing Coughing Slamming

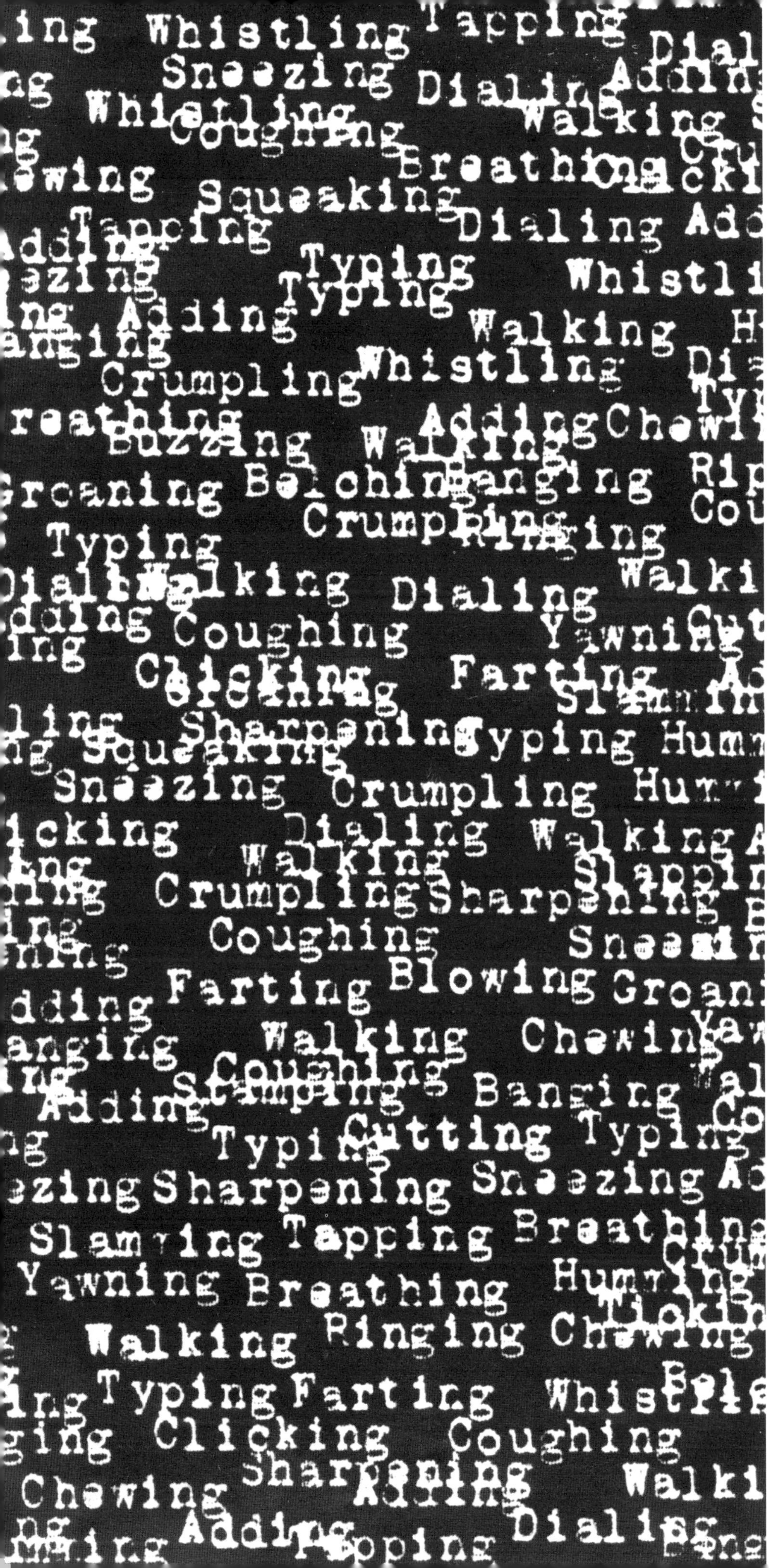

ing Whistling Tapping Dial
ng Sneezing Dialing Addin
Whistling Walking S
Coughing Cru
wing Breathing ckl
Squeaking
Tapping Dialing Add
ezing Typing Whistli
Typing Walking H
Adding Whistling Di
Crumpling
reathing Adding Chewi
Buzzing Walking
Groaning Belching anging Rip
Crumpling Cou
Typing Ringing
Dial Walking Dialing Walki
dding Coughing Yawning Cu
ing Clicking Farting Ad
ling Sharpening Typing Humm
ng Squeaking Slamming
Sneezing Crumpling Humm
icking Dialing Walking A
ing Walking Slappin
ing Crumpling Sharpening B
ing Coughing Sneez
ning Farting Blowing Groani
dding Walking Chewing Ya
anging Coughing
Adding Stamping Banging al
g Typing Cutting Typing Co
ezing Sharpening Sneezing Ad
Slamming Tapping Breathing
Yawning Breathing Humming
Walking Ringing Chewing
ing Typing Farting Whistle
ging Clicking Coughing
Chewing Sharpening Walki
ng Adding Tapping Dialing